Soups
& Starters

SARAH BROWN
A committed vegetarian, yet refreshingly undoctrinaire in her approach, Sarah Brown believes in eating good healthy food and in eating well. She gives regular demonstrations and lectures, and, as national coordinator of cookery for the Vegetarian Society of the United Kingdom, runs a series of cookery courses. Well known for her highly successful BBC television series "Vegetarian Kitchen" and for her bestselling "Sarah Brown's Vegetarian Cookbook" and "Sarah Brown's Healthy Living Cookbook", she has played a major role in promoting public awareness of the link between health and diet and the widespread move towards a healthier style of eating.

ROSELYNE MASSELIN
Roselyne Masselin was born and brought up on a farm in Normandy, France. After arriving in England six years ago, she gained extensive experience of vegetarian cooking while working in many different restaurants – including Cranks and Sarah Brown's. She then trained as a home economist and started a catering and freezer-filling business. As well as teaching cookery in Hertfordshire, where she now lives, she is a Senior Tutor for the Vegetarian Society and runs various of its courses. She is presently acting as an adviser on Food and Cookery for the Society and has appeared on television and radio on its behalf.

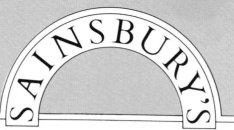

SAINSBURY'S
HEALTHY·EATING
·COOKBOOKS·

Soups
& Starters

ROSELYNE MASSELIN

SERIES·EDITOR
SARAH BROWN

CONTENTS

Soups & Starters was conceived, edited and designed by Dorling Kindersley Limited, 9 Henrietta Street, London WC2E 8PS

Published exclusively for J Sainsbury plc, Stamford House, Stamford Street, London SE1 9LL
by Dorling Kindersley Limited, 9 Henrietta Street, London WC2E 8PS

First published 1986

Copyright © 1986 by Dorling Kindersley Limited, London   Text copyright © 1986 by Sarah Elizabeth Brown Limited
Recipes by Roselyne Masselin

ISBN 0-86318-143-0

Printed in Italy

INTRODUCTION

*With a little imagination, a soup can be more than a mere prelude to a
main course. Hot or cold, light or filling, simple or ornate, soups offer
variations to suit any mood or occasion and can make an important
contribution to a healthy diet.*

WHY MAKE HOME-MADE SOUPS?

The main advantage of cooking your own soups is the huge choice of ingredients. Fresh vegetables are an excellent source of Vitamins A and C and many have a high calcium and iron content. Fresh fruit, in more unusual, sweeter soups, is rich in Vitamin C; and grains, pulses and seeds are rich in protein, B Vitamins and many minerals. All are high in fibre and do not contain artificial additives. Home-made stocks can be skimmed to remove saturated fats and cream can be replaced with low-fat alternatives. Spices and fresh herbs can be used for flavouring in place of salt.

Home-made soups need no special skill and need not be a burden on your time. Many are extremely quick and easy to concoct and can be made in advance. Most soups in this book will freeze well, so it may be worth making large quantities and freezing in batches. Home-made soups are also an inexpensive way to start a meal.

CHOOSING THE RIGHT STARTER

The vast range of ingredients available means that you can vary soups and starters according to the season and the kind of meal you are serving. A thick soup, for example, with sweet potato or pumpkin, makes an ideal winter warmer, whereas a chilled watermelon soup or a frosted fruit cocktail is more refreshing on a summer evening. Chilled soups and starters are also convenient for dinner parties and picnics when last-minute preparations are not always easy. Remember to choose a starter to balance the rest of the meal. A substantial bean, nut or pasta main course is best preceded by a light starter, whereas a high-protein soup makes a good starter before a light salad. For times when you simply want a filling one-course meal, you will find here chunky and "complete meal" soups and more filling starters that can be eaten with any of the accompaniments (see pp. 63–68).

Colour is also important, particularly when you are entertaining, and soups offer a huge choice. Beetroot, cherries and tomatoes, for example, produce wonderful shades of red, while spinach and watercress make rich, green soups. Remember, garnishes help to create contrasting colours and textures.

WHAT IS A HEALTHY DIET?

There now seems little question that good health is dependent on a healthy diet, no smoking and plenty of exercise. But what is a healthy diet? There seem to be a bewildering number of conflicting answers against a background of tempting new products, all advertised as "natural", "healthy" and "wholesome". What are the real facts?

FOOD FASHIONS

With the development of nutritional science over the last 100 years, the major nutrients – protein, fat, carbohydrate, vitamins and minerals – appear to have fallen in and out of favour. Shortly after the war, everyone was urged to eat more protein, but today we are told that the Western world consumes too much of this expensive energy source. Recently there has been a well-publicized debate about fats: is margarine better for you than butter? Carbohydrate, once the enemy of the slimming industry is now back in favour, as a result of the pro-fibre campaign. Yet sugar, another carbohydrate, has been blamed for tooth decay, obesity and adult-onset diabetes. Each of these fashions spawn a new "diet", which in turn encourages unbalanced eating.

GETTING THE BALANCE RIGHT

All the major nutrients have distinctive and important roles to play in our diet, and it is now clear that a healthy diet means eating not only the right quantity, but also the right type of each one (see pp.90–93).

The Western diet is very high in fat, sugar and salt, and low in fibre, fresh fruit and vegetables. The guidelines for a healthy diet, summed up by the reports prepared by the National Advisory Committee on Nutrition Education and the Committee on Medical Aspects of Food Policy are:

● Eat more unrefined carbohydrates which contain fibre (see pp.90–92).

● Eat more fresh fruit and vegetables, which contain fibre as well as vitamins and minerals.

● Eat less fat, sugar and salt (see pp. 90–92).

Adopting a healthy diet that will positively help your long- and short-term health is, therefore, only a shift of emphasis, which can quickly become a way of life.

WHAT IS WRONG WITH A HIGH-FAT DIET?

High-fat diets have been clearly linked with incidence of coronary heart disease. Moreover, a high-fat diet tends to be a low-fibre diet, which is associated with intestinal disorders, constipation, diverticulitis and cancer of the colon. One further danger – on a high-fat diet, it is easy to consume excess calories, as fat contains more than twice the number of calories, weight for weight, as carbohydrate and protein. Surplus fat is stored in the body as fatty deposits, which can lead to obesity and its attendant problems of diabetes, high blood pressure and gall bladder disease. It is important to cut down your fat intake to about 30–35 per cent of the day's calories or less. There are three types of fat, which need to be distinguished according to their origin and their interaction with cholesterol.

SATURATED FATS
Mainly found in foods from animal sources (particularly red meat fat, full-fat cheeses, butter and cream), saturated fats are high in cholesterol and if they are eaten in excess, the cholesterol can be laid down as fatty deposits in the blood vessels which can lead to heart disease and atherosclerosis.

POLYUNSATURATED FATS
These fats are mainly found in foods from vegetable sources in liquid oil form usually from plant seeds, such as sunflower and safflower. They are, however, also present in solid form in grains and nuts. Although they contribute to the overall fat intake, they can lower levels of cholesterol in the blood.

MONOUNSATURATED FATS

These fats, which are found in olive oil, have no effect on cholesterol levels, but do add to daily fat intake.

The three types of fat are present in varying proportions in high-fat foods. The fat in butter, for example, contains 63 per cent saturated fat and only 3 per cent polyunsaturated, whereas the fat in polyunsaturated margarine contains 65 per cent polyunsaturated and 12 per cent saturated fat.

WHAT IS WRONG WITH A SUGAR-RICH DIET?

Sugar, or sucrose, in the form of refined white or brown sugar is all too easy to eat, but contributes only calories to a diet. Sugar not used immediately for fuel is converted into fat, encouraging weight gain. Sugar is also a principle factor in tooth decay. Highly refined carbohydrates, particularly sugar are also absorbed easily into the bloodstream, quickly increasing blood sugar levels. If the body overreacts to this, the blood sugar levels drop dramatically, leaving the desire to eat something sweet and thus creating a vicious circle. In addition, the cells that produce insulin cannot always cope with sudden concentrations of glucose and diabetes may result. Try not only to cut down on sugar in drinks and cooking, but when cutting down, take particular care to avoid manufactured foods, both sweet and savoury, where sugar comes near the top of the list of ingredients. Always check the nutritional labelling on the container.

WHY DO WE NEED LESS SALT?

There is a clear link in certain people between salt intakes and high blood pressure – a condition that can lead to circulatory problems, such as heart disease and strokes. The sodium from salt works with potassium in regulating body fluids. Excess salt upsets this balance, which puts a strain on the kidneys. In general, we eat more salt than we need. Do be aware of the amount hidden in processed foods and try not to add more during home cooking.

WHAT IS SO GOOD ABOUT FIBRE?

High-fibre foods are more filling than other foods, take longer to chew and satisfy hunger for longer, which reduces the temptation to eat between meals. They are also less completely digested, thus helping to reduce actual calorie intake. The evidence strongly suggests that lack of dietary fibre can cause cancer of the colon in addition to simple constipation. A low-fibre diet often means a high-fat, high-sugar diet with the problems that induces, including adult-onset diabetes. Only plant foods, in the form of unrefined carbohydrates, like whole grains and fresh fruit and vegetables, contain fibre and it is critical to eat more. Simply switching to high-fibre breakfast cereals, from refined flours and pastas to wholemeal, in addition to eating plenty of fresh fruit and vegetables will dramatically increase your fibre intake.

Roselyne/Jarrelin

Sarah Brown

USING WHOLEFOODS

The first step in a healthy diet is to choose fresh and wholefoods that are unrefined and as close to their natural state as possible. Simply buy plenty of fresh fruit and vegetables, and use wholemeal flour, bread, pasta and pastry and health foods and whole grains, such as beans and oatmeal. When buying convenience food, select those that contain natural ingredients and the minimum of artificial colours, flavourings and preservatives. These steps alone will ensure that your diet is high in unrefined carbohydrate, rich in vitamins and minerals and lower in fat, salt and sugar.

USING THIS BOOK

The aim of this book is to translate the simple rules for health into a practical and enjoyable form. The recipes are naturally low in fat, high in fibre and unrefined ingredients, with natural sweeteners replacing sugar. Ingredients are used in their most nutritious form.

Healthy eating is not boring, nor does it involve a sacrifice. It is simply a matter of choosing and using more nutritious foods to create delicious, yet healthy meals.

USING THE RIGHT EQUIPMENT

● A blender saves a lot of time when mixing liquids or making fruit or vegetable purées. It is ideal for making soups, smooth dips and sauces.

● A food processor is more sophisticated. It comes with a variety of attachments for mincing, grating, shredding, dicing, mixing, juicing, grinding, puréeing or blending.

● If you do not have either, you will need a selection of sharp knives, an electric grinder or nut mill, a sieve, whisk, wooden spoon and mixing bowl.

● A cherry stoner and melon scoop may be useful for fruit soups and starters.

HOW TO STORE VEGETABLES

● Store in a cool, dark, dry place, since light, moisture and warmth destroy nutrients and crispness. Do not keep wrapped in polythene.

● Eat green leafy vegetables as soon as possible after purchase: courgettes, peppers, aubergines and mushrooms will keep for about 1 week in the fridge.

● Keep carrots, potatoes and onions in cool conditions for up to 3 weeks.

● The following can be stored in a freezer, after blanching. Use within a year: sweetcorn, spinach, seakale beet, broccoli, carrots, peas and green beans.

● Most vegetable purées will freeze well.

HOW TO STORE AND COOK PULSES

● Store dried beans and lentils in a cool, dry, dark place and use within 6–9 months.

● Store cooked pulses for up to 5 days in the fridge or freeze for up to 6 months.

● All pulses (except lentils and split peas) need to be soaked in cold water for 8–12 hours before cooking.

● Cook beans and whole peas in plenty of fresh water, boiling fast for the first 10 minutes, to destroy toxins. Cook most beans for about 45 minutes except black beans, butter beans, haricot beans, pinto beans and chick peas, which all need about 1 hour. Soya beans need to fast boil for a whole hour and then cook for a further 1–1½ hours. Lentils and split peas need no pre-cooking.

● The cooking liquid will make a nutritious stock for a soup.

HOW TO STORE NUTS AND SEEDS

● Store nuts in their shells where possible; they will keep for 6 months if stored in a cool place or longer, if frozen.

● Keep seeds and shelled nuts in an airtight container for not longer than 3 months. They go rancid quite quickly.

USING HERBS AND FLAVOURINGS

● Fresh herbs have a better flavour than dried, but oregano, marjoram, bay leaf, sage and dill all dry well. If you are using dried herbs instead of fresh, remember you need only half the quantity.

● Store dried herbs and all spices in airtight containers. Buy whole spices, preferably.

● Sea vegetables, such as arame and wakame, keep for up to 4 months in an airtight container once opened, or indefinitely in an unopened vacuum pack.

● Gomashio or seafood condiment can be added to soups, instead of salt.

INGREDIENTS

Part of the joy of cooking is choosing the ingredients – especially when this involves selecting fresh fruit, herbs and vegetables and trying out new, unusual and exotic foods.

Always buy the freshest ingredients possible – they contain more vitamins and minerals and have a much better flavour and texture than preserved foods. Grains, pulses, flours, cereals and dried fruit, herbs and spices, however, generally keep for at least 3 months, so it is worth maintaining a small store of basic dry ingredients, particularly those that need to be soaked or cooked in advance. It is also useful to keep a small selection of canned or bottled fruit, vegetables and beans for emergencies. But try to select those without artificial additives or a high sugar or salt content and use them by the "best before" date.

The range of "healthy" ingredients has grown dramatically in recent years, particularly low-fat, reduced sugar, reduced salt, high fibre and vegetarian alternatives to traditional foods. These open the way to both a healthier and a more varied diet and offer endless possibilities for personal variations. The success of a recipe depends as much on the quality of the raw materials as on the way you combine them. In many cases, it is better to use a fresh alternative than to use the specified ingredient if it is not at its best – use fresh, ripe peaches, for example, in place of hard or over-ripe nectarines.

The following pages illustrate many of the familiar and the unusual ingredients found in the recipes in this book – from staples, to flavourings and dairy products. The section acts as both an identification guide and a reference source. You will find advice on choosing and storing food, together with useful information about the origins, culinary applications and nutritional value of specific ingredients. For more detailed nutritional information, see pages 90–93.

VEGETABLES

The range of vegetables from Britain and abroad, now available throughout the year, is enormous. Leaf vegetables, root vegetables, shoots and sprouts are inexpensive and low in calories. They provide valuable vitamins, minerals and fibre. Buy them very fresh, store in a cool, dark place and eat as soon as possible.

MOOLI

Mooli is a mild-tasting Japanese radish that can be grated, used as a garnish, pickled or cooked like turnip.

SWEET POTATO

Sweet potato, a variety of which is known as yam, is a sweet, orange-fleshed root vegetable. Use in the same way as ordinary potato.

FENNEL

Sliced fennel resembles celery. Eat raw or cooked.

DANDELION LEAVES

An ingredient in herbal remedies and in beer and wine, dandelion leaves are also good in salad starters.

TURNIPS

Turnips are available all year. Delicious in stews and soups.

VINE LEAVES

Vine leaves are available fresh, frozen and packaged in brine.

CHICORY

Chicory is slightly bitter in taste. Eat raw or cooked.

CELERIAC

Celeriac is related to celery. Buy when firm and peel before cooking.

BEANSPROUTS

Beansprouts are an excellent source of minerals. Almost any bean or seed can be sprouted. Stir-fry, boil or eat raw.

CHINESE LEAVES

Chinese leaves have a light, crunchy texture and can be eaten raw in salads or cooked in soups.

KOHLRABI

Kohlrabi is a type of cabbage and can be purple or green. Cook like turnip.

BEETROOT

Beetroot is a very versatile root vegetable, available all year round.

MUSHROOMS

Flat, open mushrooms are the largest of a great variety of available types.

SWEETCORN

Corn on the cob is available fresh or frozen. Buy the kernels off the husk, canned or frozen.

MANGETOUT

This is a sweet variety of pea with an edible pod. They should be topped and tailed before cooking.

RADISHES

Red radish is available all year round, but tastes less peppery in the spring. Use the leaves in salad dishes.

OKRA

Okra is available fresh, canned and dried and can be eaten raw or cooked. Use as a vegetable or as a thickener.

WATERCRESS

Watercress can be used as a leaf vegetable, a herb or a garnish. Buy watercress when it is a rich green colour.

GRAINS, NUTS ～ PULSES

Grains, nuts and pulses are important sources of protein,
polyunsaturated fats, fibre and essential vitamins and minerals.
They are easy to store and, if kept in airtight containers, will keep
for several months. Pulses and grains can be cooked in large
quantities and then kept in a covered container in the fridge for
up to a week.

BARLEY FLAKES

Barley is used for cattle feed and in
the production of malt, but is also
delicious in soups and puddings. It
needs no soaking and is quick
to cook.

BUCKWHEAT

Buckwheat is a nutritious grain which is
high in iron and B Vitamins.

WHOLE WHEAT
GRAIN

The most nutritious form of
wheat and an excellent
source of protein and fibre.

OAT FLAKES

Oat flakes are a traditional northern food, most
frequently used in porridge. Oats are very rich
in protein and fibre as well as B Vitamins.

MEDIUM OATMEAL

Oatmeal comes in varying degrees of fineness and
is a good source of protein and fibre. It should not be
confused with porridge oats which
are softened and rolled.

RED KIDNEY BEANS

Red kidney beans are pleasantly sweet and
range from dark pink to maroon in colour.

SOYA BEANS

Soya beans are the most nutritious
and versatile of all the pulses.

RED SPLIT LENTILS

Red split lentils are rich in
protein and fibre.

WALNUTS

Walnuts can be used in sweet and savoury dishes. Buy them unshelled or in halves or pieces.

PINE KERNELS

Pine kernels come from the Mediterranean area. They have a mild, creamy flavour and are an excellent source of potassium, phosphorus and iron.

PISTACHIO NUTS

Pale green pistachio nuts are sold in their shells, salted and unsalted.

CASHEW NUTS

Cashew nuts have a delicate flavour and texture and can be bought loose, shelled, roasted and salted.

PECANS

Pecan nuts come from North America and are related to walnuts but have a milder flavour and are slightly less fatty. Use whole, chopped or ground.

RICE

own rice is a valuable source of fibre. absorbs more water and takes longer to cook than white rice.

SESAME SEEDS

Sesame seeds are rich in protein, calcium and phosphorus. Ground sesame seeds make a paste known as "tahini".

CHICK PEAS

Chick peas are available canned and dried. They can be sprouted and are delicious in soups and salads.

FRUIT ᴬᴺᴰ ~ FRUIT VEGETABLES

Fruit and fruit vegetables have brightly coloured skin and flesh and are visually very attractive which makes them an important ingredient in any dish. Melons and grapes are easily bruised, so handle carefully. Tree and tropical fruits are best bought slightly underripe and allowed to ripen at home. Fruit soups and cocktails make a deliciously light start to a meal.

WHITE GRAPES

Many types of grape are now readily available throughout the year. Seedless varieties are generally smaller and sweeter than seeded.

AVOCADO PEARS

An avocado is ripe when it yields all over to gentle fingertip pressure.

APPLES

Green eating apples have a sharp, clean taste and texture. They are inexpensive and available all year.

WATERMELON

Watermelon is a summer and early autumn fruit. Made of 91 per cent water, it makes a wonderfully thirst-quenching soup in the summer months.

ROCK MELON

Rock melon is available all year round. It comes from the Mediterranean in the summer months and from South Africa in the winter. Its hard skin can make it difficult to tell when it is ripe.

PINEAPPLE

A very popular tropical fruit, available all year round, fresh or canned, the pineapple is a rich source of Vitamin C.

LEMONS

Lemon rind and juice is invaluable for garnishing and flavouring sweet and savoury dishes.

LIMES

Limes are related to lemons, but are more subtle and sharper in taste.

GRAPEFRUIT

There are two main varieties of grapefruit, one with pink flesh and one with yellow. The pink-fleshed ones are much sweeter.

CHERRIES

Red cherries have a ort season, but can always be ught canned and frozen.

TOMATOES

Cherry tomatoes are miniature in size and deliciously sweet in taste. Buy them when they have a bright skin and are firm to the touch.

ORANGES

Oranges are available with or without seeds. All types are rich in Vitamin C.

PEPPERS

Peppers are rich in Vitamin C and come in a variety of colours, shapes and sizes. They are available all year round and can be eaten raw or cooked.

AUBERGINE

Aubergines come in a variety of sizes, shapes and colours, but are usually oval in shape, with a glossy purple skin and creamy flesh. Fresh aubergines are available all year round.

PUMPKIN

Pumpkins have a distinctive orange skin and fibrous flesh and make a satisfying soup.

SPICES AND FLAVOURINGS

The final touch to any dish is the seasoning and there is now a wide range of spices and flavourings available. Clever use of these ingredients can make all the difference, giving a bland soup or insipid starter an unusual, exciting taste.

NUTMEG

Buy fresh, whole nutmeg, as the aroma diminishes when ground.

ALLSPICE

These berries taste of cloves, cinnamon and nutmeg.

TAHINI

Tahini is a paste made fro ground sesame seeds. Hig in protein and calcium, makes a tasty dip.

MACE

Mace is the husk of nutmeg.

DRIED CHESTNUTS

Chestnuts are available fresh in the winter and dried, canned and puréed all year.

ROOT GINGER

Root ginger is available fresh and dried. Peel and grate before use.

CINNAMON

Use cinnamon in sweet soups and starters.

HONEY

Honey is a natural sweetener.

DRIED MUSHROOMS

Mushrooms are a good source of potassium and sodium. Soak dried ones in tepid water to reconstitute.

NASTURTIUM

Nasturtium leaves, flowers and seeds are all edible. The peppery taste is ideal in salads and starters.

DIJON MUSTARD

Dijon mustard is hot, ideal for spicing up mild soups or giving a light dressing extra tang.

WAKAME

Wakame is an extremely nutritious sea vegetable containing valuable minerals, vitamins and protein.

KOMBU

Kombu is a sea vegetable, and an excellent source of minerals, B Vitamins and protein.

SHOYU

Shoyu is a naturally fermented sauce made from soya beans.

TABASCO

Tabasco is a hot relish which lends a spicy flavour to Mexican-style dishes.

CURRY LEAVES

Curry leaves can be bought fresh or dried and used in any curry dish.

ARAME

Arame is a mild tasting sea vegetable and is rich in iron.

HORSERADISH

Horseradish is a spicy sauce made from grated horseradish and fresh or sour cream. A good source of Vitamin C.

AGAR-AGAR FLAKES

Agar-agar is a sea vegetable derivative, available in flake or powder form and an ideal healthy alternative to gelatine in jellied soups, mousses and pâtés.

MISO

Miso is a fermented soya bean product. Its salty taste goes well in Oriental-type soups.

HERBS

Herbs are a valuable source of vitamins and minerals in soups and starters, and contribute a wide variety of natural flavours. Fresh herbs have a fuller taste and make a more attractive garnish than dried. Store dried herbs in an airtight container.

LOVAGE

Lovage tastes like celery and parsley combined. Use as a garnish, or to add flavour to soups and salads.

DILL

Fresh dill, or dill weed, combines well with vegetable soups and salads.

DILL SEEDS

Dill seeds taste rather like caraway and go well in garnishes, sauces and pickles.

POPPY SEED

Poppy seeds are nativ the Middle East and used in Indian and Je cooking. They are wh bluish black.

CELERY SEEDS

Celery seeds have a slightly bitter taste which goes well with egg- and salad-based starters.

JUNIPER

Juniper berries have a pungent flavour which will lighten a rich soup.

GREEN PEPPERCORNS

The berries of the pepper plant, usually pickled in brine.

BLACK MUSTARD SEEDS

Black mustard seeds are stronger than white ones.

CAPERS

Capers are usually sold pi in vinegar and should no allowed to dry out. The well in soups and sauce

BASIL

Fresh basil is a very versatile herb which combines well with garlic in soups and sauces.

BLACK PEPPERCORNS

Black peppercorns can be ground or used whole.

FRENCH PARSLEY

French parsley has flat leaves, a delicate flavour and a gentle, pervasive aroma.

ENGLISH PARSLEY

English parsley has curled leaves and is an excellent source of Vitamin C and iron.

DRIED PARSLEY

Dried parsley is excellent for flavouring soups and starters.

CHERVIL

Chervil has a delicate flavour which is destroyed by cooking. Use like parsley.

THYME

Thyme is a popular herb, containing an oil which aids the digestion of fatty foods. It mixes well with other herbs.

BOUQUET GARNI

Bouquet garni – mixed dried herbs wrapped in muslin or a sachet – adds a rich flavour.

SAVORY

Savory has a distinctive peppery taste and combines well with bean-based dishes.

SAGE

Sage combines well with pea- and bean-based soups.

ROSEMARY

Rosemary, an aromatic Mediterranean herb, combines well with beans and vegetables.

MINT

Mint has a clean, fresh taste which complements light soups, fruit-based starters, simple mousses, sorbets and leafy salad vegetables.

CORIANDER

Ground coriander is mild but aromatic and is important in Eastern food.

CORIANDER

Coriander is mild and aromatic and an important ingredient in Eastern food. The leaves make an attractive garnish.

DAIRY PRODUCTS AND ALTERNATIVES

Dairy products have an important part to play in a healthy diet because they are a valuable source of protein and calcium. Low-fat cheeses and yogurt contribute these nutrients without adding too many calories or saturated fats. There are also various soya-based alternatives to dairy products as well as rennet-free vegetarian cheeses, which are readily available.

FIRM TOFU

Firm tofu is hard-pressed soya bean curd and a valuable source of protein.

SOUR CREAM

Sour cream has a smooth texture and fresh taste which is delicious in soups and sauces.

YOGURT

Yogurt is available either full-fat or low-fat and is an excellent source of protein and calcium.

BUTTERMILK

Buttermilk is a low-fat milk often used in baking.

SILKEN TOFU

Silken tofu is a curd made from lightly-pressed soya milk. It is very versatile and is a good substitute for cream – ideal in soups and sauces.

SMETANA

Smetana, made with skimmed milk, is a low-fat substitute for cream.

SMOKED TOFU

Smoked tofu is made from smoked soya bean curd. It has a subtle flavour and is a rich source of protein.

VEGETARIAN CHEDDAR

Vegetarian Cheddar cheese is made with a vegetable version of the rennet used in the manufacture of cheese. It has the same amount of fat and protein as ordinary Cheddar, and contains useful vitamins and minerals.

FETA

Feta is a moist, crumbly Greek cheese made from sheep's or goat's milk. It has a sharp, tangy taste.

RICOTTA

Ricotta is a mild, unripened Italian cheese with a light, creamy taste, which is made from the whey of cow's or goat's milk.

SOUPS

A soup can be a meal in itself or a light appetizer before a main course. But whatever the consistency, if you use fresh, wholesome ingredients it will add valuable nutrients to your diet. This section includes soups for all moods and occasions – hot, cold, clear, smooth, chunky – and you can always use more or less liquid according to your taste.

RAW VEGETABLE SOUP

INGREDIENTS

¹/₂ bunch watercress, chopped
1 large avocado, peeled, stoned and chopped
¹/₂ medium green pepper, deseeded and chopped
1 green eating apple, cored and chopped
12 fl oz (350ml) water
1 vegetable stock cube
juice of ¹/₂ lemon
1 tsp (5ml) chopped fresh lovage

GARNISH
cress, chopped parsley or lovage, or a few sprigs of watercress

•

NUTRITION PROFILE

A good source of Vitamins C and E, this soup also contains folic acid.

• Per portion •
Carbohydrate: 4.1g
Protein: 2.4g   **Fibre:** 1.8g
Fat: 10.6g   **Calories:** 120

This fresh green potage is best eaten as soon as it is made to conserve all the vitamins. When chopping the watercress, be sure to discard the large stalks, which taste very peppery.

Preparation time: 10–15 mins
Serves 4

METHOD

1. Put all the soup ingredients except the lovage in a blender or food processor and mix for a few seconds until just smooth.

2. Pour out of the blender into a serving bowl and stir in the lovage.

3. Garnish and serve in cool soup bowls.

Illustrated on page 23

BEETROOT AND ORANGE SOUP

INGREDIENTS

6oz (175g) raw beetroot, peeled
and diced
½ pint (300ml) red grape juice
juice of 2 oranges
4oz (125g) smetana
½ tsp ground allspice

•

NUTRITION PROFILE

*This low-fat, low-calorie soup is a good
source of Vitamin C.*

• Per portion •
Carbohydrate: 15.4g
Protein: 2.2g **Fibre:** 1.6g
Fat: 2.9g **Calories:** 95

*Orange and beetroot make a delicious and nutritious combination in
this colourful soup. Raw beetroot contains valuable supplies of minerals
and those that are hard to the touch contain most moisture and juice. A
garnish of orange slices goes well with this soup.*

Preparation time: 20 mins (plus chilling time)
Serves 4

METHOD

1. In a juicer, blender or food processor, mix the beetroot and red
grape juice until smooth. If you are not using a juicer, sieve the
mixture through a double layer of muslin or a tea towel.

2. Blend the juice with the orange juice, smetana and allspice for
a few seconds in the washed blender or food processor.

3. Chill for 2–3 hours before serving.

Illustrated opposite

RAW CARROT AND PINEAPPLE SOUP

INGREDIENTS

8oz (250g) carrots, scrubbed and diced
4oz (125g) fresh pineapple flesh
12 fl oz (350ml) water
2 tbsp (30ml) lemon juice
1 pear or apple, peeled, cored and diced
2 tsp (10ml) chopped apple mint

GARNISH
a few apple mint leaves
a few thin slices of pear or apple

•

NUTRITION PROFILE

*This fat-free, low-calorie soup is rich in
Vitamins A and C.*

• Per portion •
Carbohydrate: 10g
Protein: 0.7g **Fibre:** 2.7g
Fat: -- **Calories:** 40

*This cool, fruity soup makes a healthy start to any meal. There are
many types of mint; here apple mint adds a little sharpness to the sweet
fruity flavour and makes a good garnish. When blending the carrot and
pineapple, you will need to process the ingredients several times to get a
smooth result.*

Preparation time: 25 mins (plus chilling time)
Serves 4

METHOD

1. In a juicer, blender or food processor, mix the carrot and
pineapple together until very smooth. If you are not using a
juicer, sieve the mixture through a double layer of muslin
or a tea towel.

2. Add the water, lemon juice and pear or apple and blend again.

3. Transfer the soup to a bowl and add the chopped apple mint.
Chill for 2–3 hours.

4. Garnish with apple mint leaves and pear or apple slices.
Serve cold.

Illustrated opposite

Clockwise from top: **Raw vegetable soup** (*see p. 21*); **Raw carrot and pineapple soup** (*see above*);
Beetroot and orange soup (*see above*).

HUNGARIAN CUCUMBER SOUP

INGREDIENTS

6 fl oz (175ml) buttermilk
6 fl oz (175ml) natural yogurt
$\frac{1}{2}$ large or $\frac{3}{4}$ small cucumber
$\frac{1}{2}$ tsp cider vinegar
$\frac{1}{2}$ tsp dill seeds
$\frac{1}{2}$ tsp fresh dill weed
1 tbsp (15ml) chopped fresh mint

•

NUTRITION PROFILE

This low-fat and low-calorie soup is rich in Vitamin B_2 and calcium.

• Per portion •
Carbohydrate: 4.6g
Protein: 3.2g **Fibre:** 0.3g
Fat: 0.4g **Calories:** 35

This cooling, dill-flavoured soup, ideal for hot summer days, contains the thirst-quenching combination of yogurt and cucumber. For added taste, fibre and colour, do not peel the cucumber.

Preparation time: 20 mins (plus chilling time)
Serves 4

METHOD

1. Mix the buttermilk and yogurt together.

2. Chop half the cucumber into small cubes. Grate the remainder, using the coarser side of the grater, or the grating disc of a processor. Set on one side.

3. In a blender or food processor, mix the cubed cucumber with the cider vinegar and dill seeds until smooth. Add to the buttermilk mixture.

4. Stir in the dill, mint and grated cucumber, mixing well. Serve chilled. Add an ice cube on very hot days.

Illustrated on page 26

GAZPACHO

INGREDIENTS

1 large red pepper
1 pint (600ml) tomato juice
2 tbsp (30ml) red wine vinegar
2oz (50g) wholemeal breadcrumbs
1 tsp (5ml) clear honey
1 small clove garlic, crushed

GARNISH
8oz (250g) tomatoes, diced
$\frac{1}{2}$ cucumber, diced
$\frac{1}{2}$ green pepper, deseeded and diced

•

NUTRITION PROFILE

This low-fat, low-calorie soup is a good source of Vitamins A, B_1, B_6, C and E, folic acid and iron.

• Per portion •
Carbohydrate: 15.2g
Protein: 3.7g **Fibre:** 2.8g
Fat: 0.6g **Calories:** 80

Gazpacho is a traditional Spanish cold soup, served with a variety of raw vegetables (see p. 67). The authentic version is made with olive oil, while this version is virtually free from fat and low in calories. You can remove pepper skins by baking or grilling.

Preparation time: 15 mins (plus chilling time)   Cooking time: 20 mins
Serves 4

METHOD

1. Put the red pepper in an ovenproof dish and cook in a preheated oven at Gas Mark 5, 375°F, 190°C for 20 minutes.

2. Cool slightly and peel off the skin. Halve and deseed the pepper, then purée the flesh with the tomato juice, red wine vinegar, breadcrumbs, honey and garlic in a blender or food processor.

3. Chill thoroughly. Just before serving, fold in the diced tomatoes, cucumber and green pepper.

Illustrated on page 26

CHILLED SOUR CHERRY SOUP

INGREDIENTS

1 lb (500g) Morello cherries
7 fl oz (200ml) white grape juice
fl oz (200ml) medium-dry white wine
1 inch (2.5cm) cinnamon stick
rind and juice of ½ lemon
5oz (150g) carton natural yogurt
2 tbsp (30ml) sour cream

GARNISH

2 tbsp (30ml) sour cream

•

NUTRITION PROFILE

This soup is a good source of calcium.

• Per portion •
Carbohydrate: 25.8g
Protein: 3.4g **Fibre:** 2.1g
Fat: 3.6g **Calories:** 175

Dark, plump Morello cherries provide the best colour and flavour for this soup. The natural yogurt helps to offset the acidity of the lemon and grape juice, while the sour cream complements the taste of the fruit. A few stoned cherries also make a nice garnish.

Preparation time: 20 mins (plus chilling time)   Cooking time: 15 mins
Serves 4

METHOD

1. Remove the cherry stalks and put on one side. Prepare the cherries (see below).

2. Add the grape juice, wine, cinnamon, lemon rind and juice to the cherry stalks and stones and cook (see below).

3. Blend the cherries with the liquid (see below) in a blender or food processor. Pour in the yogurt and sour cream and process for another few seconds. Leave to cool, then cover and refrigerate until ready to serve.

4. Serve chilled, garnished with some cherries (optional) and a swirl of sour cream.

Illustrated on page 26

MAKING CHERRY SAUCE

There are several hundred varieties of cherry. The best known sour cherries are morellos (with dark or light skins) and amarelles (with red skins). A basic cherry purée is extremely versatile and can be used as the base for a soup, as here, as a topping for fruit desserts, pancakes or healthy ice creams, or as a base for sauces or mousses. Cherries have rather a short season, but you can use canned or frozen ones.

1. Stone the cherries using either a cherry stoner or the tip of a pointed knife, and set on one side.

2. Simmer the stalks and stones with the liquids for 5 minutes. Cool, then strain and blend until smooth.

3. Combine the cherry purée with the yogurt and sour cream (as above). Process for a few more seconds.

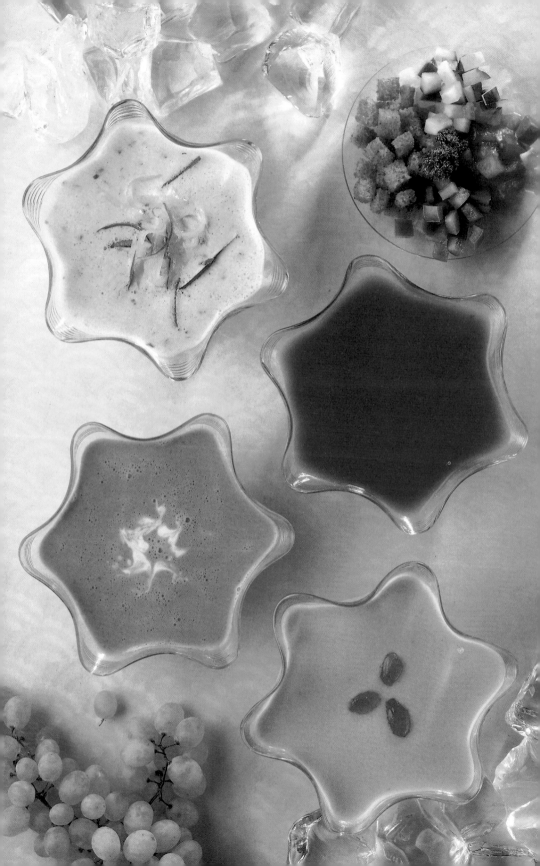

CHILLED GRAPE AND CASHEW NUT SOUP

INGREDIENTS

8oz (250g) unsalted cashew nuts
1 lb (500g) seedless white grapes
8 fl oz (250ml) water

GARNISH

4oz (125g) seedless white grapes,
halved lengthways

•

NUTRITION PROFILE

Rich in protein and fibre, this soup is a good source of Vitamins B_1 and C, magnesium and iron.

• Per portion •
Carbohydrate: 42.6g
Protein: 11.7g **Fibre:** 5.7g
Fat: 28.6g **Calories:** 450

A garnish of seedless grapes gives this sweet, nutty soup added sharpness and texture. The cashew nuts are a good source of protein and fat, so for a good balance, this soup is best followed by a grain dish.

Preparation time: 25 mins (plus chilling time)
Serves 4

METHOD

1. Grind 2oz (50g) cashew nuts at a time in a small electric grinder or food processor to form a smooth paste.

2. Purée the ground nuts and grapes in a blender or food processor until smooth.

3. Add the water and blend again.

4. Chill before serving and garnish with the grape halves.

Illustrated opposite

CHILLED WATERMELON SOUP

INGREDIENTS

½ large watermelon (about
3 lb/1.5kg in weight), deseeded
juice of 1 lemon
4–6 cloves

GARNISH

a few ice cubes
nasturtium flowers

•

NUTRITION PROFILE

This fat-free and low-calorie soup is a useful source of iron and Vitamin C.

• Per portion •
Carbohydrate: 10.1g
Protein: 0.8g **Fibre:** 2.3g
Fat: –– **Calories:** 40

This stunning, colourful soup makes an attractive starter for a summer evening dinner party. It is light, refreshing and low in calories. It is also quick and easy to prepare. If nasturtium flowers are not available, garnish with watercress.

Preparation time: 15 mins (plus chilling time)
Serves 4

METHOD

1. Using a small scoop or spoon, scoop out several melon balls from the watermelon and reserve for decoration. Scoop out the rest of the flesh and put on one side.

2. Scrape the inner sides of the melon until smooth.

3. In a blender or food processor, mix the melon flesh with the lemon juice until smooth.

4. Pour the mixture into the melon shell, add the cloves and the melon balls and refrigerate.

5. Add a few ice cubes and garnish with nasturtium flowers.

Illustrated on page 29

Clockwise from top left: **Hungarian cucumber soup** (*see p. 24*); **Gazpacho** (*see p. 24*);
Chilled grape and cashew nut soup (*see above*); **Chilled sour cherry soup** (*see p. 25*).

CHILLED COURGETTE ~ TARRAGON SOUP

INGREDIENTS

1 pint (600ml) clear light
stock or water
1oz (25g) fresh tarragon
2 tsp (10ml) sunflower oil
6 spring onions, trimmed and chopped
8oz (250g) courgettes, sliced
1 tsp (5ml) aniseed, crushed
8 nasturtium leaves, finely chopped
1/2–3/4 tsp agar-agar powder
1 tsp (5ml) lemon juice
salt and black pepper
1 kiwi fruit, sliced

GARNISH
slices of kiwi fruit

•

NUTRITION PROFILE

*This soup is low in fat and calories and a
good source of iron and Vitamins B₁ and C.*

• Per portion •
Carbohydrate: 6.7g
Protein: 1.5g **Fibre:** 1.8g
Fat: 3g **Calories:** 60

*This delicately flavoured soup is light and refreshing in hot weather.
Agar-agar is a jelling agent made from a sea vegetable or seaweed, and
comes in flakes or a more concentrated powder form.*

Preparation time: 25 mins (plus 2–3 hours' setting time)
Cooking time: 10–15 mins
Serves 4

METHOD

1. Put the stock in a saucepan and bring to the boil. Remove from
the heat and add the tarragon. Leave to infuse for 5 minutes.
Strain, reserving the flavoured stock.

2. Heat the oil in a medium saucepan and gently fry the spring
onions for 1–2 minutes. Add the courgettes and fry until most of
them have changed colour.

3. Add the aniseeds and nasturtium leaves and cook for 30
seconds, stirring. Add the tarragon stock, bring to the boil and
simmer for 4–5 minutes.

4. Sprinkle the agar-agar powder over the soup and stir until
dissolved. Simmer for a further 1–2 minutes.

5. Add the lemon juice, seasoning and the kiwi fruit. Leave to
cool and pour into serving dishes or glasses. Refrigerate for a few
hours. Garnish each glass with a slice of kiwi fruit or nasturtium
leaves and serve chilled.

Illustrated opposite

BASIC WHITE STOCK

INGREDIENTS

1½ pints (900ml) water
½ onion, peeled and chopped
1 medium carrot, scrubbed and
chopped
handful celery leaves
few black peppercorns

•

NUTRITION PROFILE

*This basic white stock is rich in Vitamins A
and D but does not contain significant
amounts of other nutrients.*

*Stocks form a useful starch-free base for many soups, adding flavour
and colour as well as body. This recipe makes a simple, clear stock,
although any vegetable leaves, stems, roots and shoots can be used. To
make a tomato-flavoured stock, add 2 tsp (10ml) tomato purée.*

Preparation time: 5 mins Cooking time: 8 mins
Makes 1½ pints (900ml)

METHOD

1. Place all the ingredients in a medium saucepan.

2. Bring to the boil and simmer for 7–8 minutes. Strain and use.

Illustrated on page 32

Top: **Chilled courgette and tarragon soup** (*see above*); Bottom: **Chilled watermelon soup** (*see p.27*).

DARK STOCK

INGREDIENTS

¼oz (7g) dried mushrooms
1 strip kombu (or wakame or arame)
1½ pints (900ml) cold water
2 tbsp (30ml) buckwheat
1 medium carrot, scrubbed
and chopped
few black peppercorns

•

NUTRITION PROFILE

This dark stock is a good source of iron, iodine and B Vitamins but does not contain significant amounts of other nutrients.

Sea vegetables are an excellent stock base. They contain valuable vitamins and minerals and add a strong flavour and colour. Dried mushrooms also contribute a rich natural flavour and the roasted buckwheat gives a nutty taste.

Preparation time: 10 mins   Cooking time: 10 mins
Makes 1½ pints (900ml)

METHOD

1. Soak the mushrooms and kombu in the cold water for a few minutes.

2. Meanwhile roast the buckwheat in a heavy-based saucepan until a roasted aroma rises and the buckwheat becomes a slightly deeper shade.

3. After 2–3 minutes, add the mushrooms and kombu, together with the soaking water.

4. Add the carrot and peppercorns, bring to the boil and simmer for 7–8 minutes.

5. Strain and use within a day.

Illustrated on page 32

MAKING DARK STOCK

Vegetarian stocks are as rich in flavour and as wholesome as meat-based ones and can be adapted for use in sauces, soups and casseroles. Any cooking liquid from beans, grains or vegetables can be used, but green vegetables can give too strong a flavour. Sea vegetables make an excellent base for a rich dark stock. Red or black beans also make good dark stock, while white beans or chick peas make tasty pale stock.

1. Soak the dried vegetables and seaweed in 1½ pints (900ml) cold water for a few minutes.

2. Roast 2 tbsp (30ml) buckwheat in a heavy-based saucepan for 2–3 minutes, until a roasted aroma rises.

3. Add the rehydrated vegetables and their soaking water to the buckwheat. Add the seasoning and any other vegetables. Simmer for 7–8 minutes. Strain and use within one day.

QUICK STOCKS

The following are quick and easy methods of making stock. Some may change the colour of the soup, so choose your method carefully.

- Dissolve 2 tsp (10ml) miso in 1 pint (600ml) hot water.
- Dissolve 1 tsp (5ml) vegetable concentrate in 1 pint (600ml) hot water.
- Dissolve 1 tsp (5ml) yeast extract in 1 pint (600ml) hot water.
- Dissolve 1 vegetable stock cube in 1 pint (600ml) hot water.
- Add 2 tsp (10ml) shoyu or tamari to 1 pint (600ml) water.

CONSOMME JULIENNE

INGREDIENTS
2oz (50g) carrots, scrubbed
2oz (50g) turnips, scrubbed
2oz (50g) celery, trimmed
2oz (50g) green cabbage
1½ pints (900ml) light stock
1 bay leaf
salt and black pepper

•

NUTRITION PROFILE
This fat-free and very low-calorie soup is rich in Vitamins A and C.

• Per portion •
Carbohydrate: 1.8g
Protein: 0.5g **Fibre:** 1.3g
Fat: –– **Calories:** 10

Consommé is a light clear soup which makes an excellent appetizer before a large main course. It is very light and full of flavour and contains many valuable nutrients. The vegetables, when cut into julienne strips, look attractive and provide texture.

Preparation time: 10 mins   Cooking time: 15 mins
Serves 4

METHOD

1. Cut the vegetables into julienne (long, thin) strips.

2. Place the stock in a saucepan and bring to the boil. Add the vegetables and bay leaf and simmer for 10–15 minutes or until the vegetables are just tender.

3. Remove the bay leaf, season to taste and serve immediately.

Illustrated on page 32

CONSOMME WITH FLORETS

INGREDIENTS

1½ pints (900ml) light stock
2oz (50g) peas
2oz (50g) cauliflower florets, broken
into small pieces
2oz (50g) carrots, scrubbed and sliced
2oz (50g) French beans, finely chopped
1 bouquet garni
salt and black pepper

•

NUTRITION PROFILE

*Rich in Vitamins A and C, this soup is also
fat-free and low in calories.*

• Per portion •
Carbohydrate: 2.4g
Protein: 1.1g   **Fibre:** 1.7g
Fat: --   **Calories:** 15

*The bouquet garni gives a pervasive taste of herbs in this light and
healthy consommé. If you grow your own herbs, you could make a
bouquet garni by simply tying together a few sprigs of parsley, a sprig of
thyme, a small bay leaf and any other herbs you like.*

Preparation time: 5 mins   Cooking time: 15 mins
Serves 4

METHOD

1. Place the stock in a saucepan and bring to the boil. Add the
vegetables and bouquet garni.

2. Simmer for 15 minutes or until the vegetables are tender.

3. Remove the bouquet garni, season to taste and serve hot.

Illustrated opposite

VERMICELLI CONSOMME

INGREDIENTS

1¼ pints (750ml) light stock
2 tsp (10ml) tomato purée
2oz (50g) vermicelli
1 red or green pepper, deseeded
and diced
1 carrot, peeled and diced
1 tsp (5ml) green peppercorns, crushed
1 tsp (5ml) chopped fresh chervil
salt and black pepper

•

NUTRITION PROFILE

*This low-calorie soup is a good source of
Vitamins A and C and contains
very little fat.*

• Per portion •
Carbohydrate: 11.3g
Protein: 1.6g   **Fibre:** 0.7g
Fat: 0.2g   **Calories:** 55

*This traditional Italian consommé is light, full of flavour and a little
more substantial than vegetable-based consommés. Small pasta shapes
could be substituted for vermicelli. Green peppercorns, the unripe
berries of the familiar black peppercorns, are usually pickled in brine
and add to the flavour.*

Preparation time: 10 mins   Cooking time: 18 mins
Serves 4

METHOD

1. Put the stock in a saucepan and bring to the boil. Add the
tomato purée and vermicelli and simmer for a few seconds.

2. Stir in the pepper, carrot and peppercorns and simmer for
15 minutes.

3. Add the chopped chervil and season to taste. Serve hot.

Illustrated opposite

Clockwise from top left: **Vermicelli consommé** (*see above*); **Dark stock** (*see p.30*); **Basic white stock** (*see p.28*);
Consommé with florets (*see above*); **Consommé julienne** (*see p.31*).

EGG FLOWER SOUP

INGREDIENTS

1½ pints (900ml) well-flavoured
light stock
1 tbsp (15ml) soya sauce
1 tsp (5ml) lemon juice
2 tsp (10ml) fresh ginger root, peeled
and grated
2 eggs, beaten
6 spring onions, trimmed and chopped
1–2 tbsp (15–30ml) chopped
fresh parsley
1oz (25g) cooked sweetcorn
salt and black pepper
•

NUTRITION PROFILE

*This low-calorie soup is a good source of
Vitamins B$_{12}$, C and D.*

• Per portion •
Carbohydrate: 3.2g
Protein: 3.6g **Fibre:** 1.1g
Fat: 2.8g **Calories:** 55

*This is a vegetarian adaptation of a Chinese soup, in which the eggs are
stirred into the soup to form strands resembling a flower. The
traditional meat stock is here replaced by vegetable stock and plenty of
seasoning.*

Preparation time: 10 mins   Cooking time: 5–10 mins
Serves 4

METHOD

1. Put the stock in a large saucepan and bring to the boil. Stir in
the soya sauce, lemon juice and ginger.

2. Just before serving, pour on the beaten eggs and slowly stir into
the boiling soup.

3. When the eggs have set and formed strands, remove the soup
from the heat. Add the spring onions, parsley and sweetcorn.
Season to taste and serve immediately.

Illustrated opposite

CELERY AND TOMATO SOUP

INGREDIENTS

2 tsp (10ml) olive oil
1 onion, peeled and finely chopped
6 sticks celery, trimmed and chopped
1 clove garlic, crushed
pinch salt
6 large tomatoes, skinned, deseeded
and chopped
1 tbsp (15ml) chopped fresh parsley
1 tbsp (15ml) fresh basil
1 pint (600ml) stock or water
salt and black pepper
•

NUTRITION PROFILE

*Low in calories, this soup is a good
source of Vitamin C.*

• Per portion •
Carbohydrate: 4.2g
Protein: 1.2g **Fibre:** 1.9g
Fat: 2.5g **Calories:** 45

*This strongly flavoured, colourful soup makes a great summer starter
and is delicious served with crusty bread (see p.64) or cheese rusks
(see p.66). The tomatoes can be deseeded, but leaving them whole
increases the fibre content. A garnish of chopped fresh parsley goes
well with this soup.*

Preparation time: 15 mins   Cooking time: 25 mins
Serves 4

METHOD

1. Heat the oil in a large saucepan and gently fry the onion.

2. Add the celery and garlic, sprinkle them with a pinch of salt to
bring out the juices and cook for 10 minutes.

3. Add the tomatoes to the pan with the parsley, basil and stock.
Simmer for 15 minutes.

4. Season to taste and serve.

Illustrated opposite

From top: **Celery and tomato soup** (*see above*); **Egg flower soup** (*see above*); **Winter vegetable soup** (*see p. 36*).

WINTER VEGETABLE SOUP

INGREDIENTS

1 tbsp (15ml) sunflower oil
4oz (125g) onion, peeled and chopped
2 tsp (10ml) fresh sage
2 tsp (10ml) fresh rosemary
1 bay leaf
2oz (50g) swede, scrubbed and diced
2oz (50g) turnip, scrubbed and diced
2oz (50g) winter radish, cut into strips
4oz (125g) carrots, scrubbed and diced
4oz (125g) winter cabbage, chopped
1¾ pints (1 litre) stock or water
1 vegetable stock cube
salt and black pepper

•

NUTRITION PROFILE

*This low-calorie soup is rich in Vitamins
A, C and E.*

• Per portion •
Carbohydrate: 5.6g
Protein: 1.7g **Fibre:** 3.2g
Fat: 3.9g **Calories:** 65

A selection of inexpensive winter vegetables makes a warming, chunky soup for cold days. Other root vegetables and herbs can be substituted, according to preference and availability.

Preparation time: 15 mins   Cooking time: 1 hour
Serves 4

METHOD

1. Heat the oil in a saucepan and gently fry the onion until soft. Add the sage, rosemary and bay leaf and fry for a further 1–2 minutes.

2. Stir in the swede, turnip, winter radish and carrots and cook for another 5 minutes or until the vegetables are golden.

3. Add the cabbage, stock and stock cube. Cover and cook for 40–50 minutes. Remove the bay leaf, season to taste and serve hot.

Illustrated on page 35

MISO SOUP WITH ARAME ᴬᴺᴰ BROCCOLI

INGREDIENTS

¼oz (7g) arame
1¾ pints (1 litre) dark stock or water
1 small onion, peeled and sliced
1 medium carrot, peeled and cut
into matchsticks
3oz (75g) broccoli spears, broken up
into small pieces
2oz (50g) white cabbage, cut into
thin strips
1–2 tbsp (15–30ml) miso

•

NUTRITION PROFILE

*This fat-free and low-calorie soup is rich in
Vitamins A and C.*

• Per portion •
Carbohydrate: 5.1g
Protein: 1.2g **Fibre:** 1.7g
Fat: –– **Calories:** 25

Miso is fermented from soya beans and contains bacteria and live enzymes that are beneficial to the digestive system, but destroyed by cooking. Hatcho miso, a pure soya product with a strong flavour, is used here, but mugi miso (with a mellower flavour) can be substituted.

Preparation time: 10 mins   Cooking time: 10 mins
Serves 4

METHOD

1. Soak the arame in the stock or water in a large saucepan for a few minutes.

2. Add all the other ingredients, except the miso, bring to the boil and simmer for 8–10 minutes or until the vegetables are tender.

3. Cool slightly, dissolve the miso in the soup and serve.

Illustrated on page 38

LETTUCE AND SORREL SOUP
WITH PEPPERMINT

INGREDIENTS

7 fl oz (200ml) apple juice
7 fl oz (200ml) water
$\frac{1}{2}$ tsp peppermint tea leaves
$\frac{1}{2}$ crisp apple, diced
$\frac{1}{4}$ cucumber, diced
$\frac{1}{2}$oz (15g) sorrel, shredded
4oz (125g) crisp lettuce, shredded
$\frac{1}{2}$ tsp lemon juice

•

NUTRITION PROFILE

This low-fat, low-calorie starter is a good source of Vitamin C.

• Per portion •
Carbohydrate: 6.9g
Protein: 0.9g **Fibre:** 0.9g
Fat: 0.2g **Calories:** 35

This unusual soup is delightfully refreshing, easy to digest and is equally good served hot or chilled. Sorrel, high in oxalic acid, brings a fresh, sharp contrast to the sweetness of the fruity base.

Preparation time: 15 mins   Cooking time: 10 mins
Serves 4

METHOD

1. Put the apple juice and water into a saucepan and bring to the boil. Remove from the heat, add the peppermint tea leaves and allow to infuse for 6 minutes.

2. Drain the mixture through muslin and reserve the juice. Pour the juice into a small saucepan and reheat gently. Bring to the boil, add the apple and cucumber and simmer for 3–5 minutes.

3. Add the sorrel, lettuce and lemon juice. Bring back to the boil and serve straight away or chill and serve cold.

Illustrated on page 38

SOUP CHINESE STYLE

INGREDIENTS

2 tsp (10ml) sesame oil
1 inch (2.5cm) piece of fresh root ginger, peeled and grated
$\frac{1}{2}$ onion, peeled and sliced
2oz (50g) mushrooms, wiped and sliced
1$\frac{3}{4}$ pints (1 litre) stock
2 leaves Chinese cabbage, shredded
2 inch (5cm) mooli, thinly sliced
1oz (25g) Chinese noodles
4oz (125g) soft tofu, cut into strips
2oz (50g) beansprouts
2 tsp–1 tbsp (10–15ml) tamari or shoyu

•

NUTRITION PROFILE

This low-calorie soup is rich in calcium and copper.

• Per portion•
Carbohydrate: 7.3g
Protein: 4.2g **Fibre:** 0.9g
Fat: 4.5g **Calories:** 85

The rich variety of oriental vegetables gives this soup an exotic appeal and a good balance of essential nutrients. The tofu adds protein and a smooth texture, while the ginger and tamari, a naturally fermented soya sauce, contribute to the subtle flavours. Mooli, a large white radish, is also known as daikon or Japanese white radish.

Preparation time: 15 mins   Cooking time: 10 mins
Serves 4

METHOD

1. Heat the oil in a heavy-based saucepan and fry the ginger and onion for 1–2 minutes.

2. Add the mushrooms and cook for a further 2 minutes. Add the stock and bring to the boil. Stir in the Chinese cabbage and the mooli and cook for 3–4 minutes.

3. Add the noodles, tofu and beansprouts, bring back to the boil and remove from the heat. Stir in the tamari, cover and leave to stand for 6 minutes before serving.

Illustrated on page 38

BEETROOT AND TURNIP SOUP
WITH HORSERADISH

INGREDIENTS

6oz (175g) beetroot, peeled and diced
6oz (175g) baby turnips, diced
1 pint (600ml) light stock or water
2 tsp (10ml) fresh thyme
1 bouquet garni
1 tsp (5ml) prepared mustard
1 tbsp (15ml) creamed horseradish
1 tbsp (15ml) lemon juice
1 tsp (5ml) yeast extract
1 tsp (5ml) arrowroot
salt and black pepper

GARNISH
1 small red onion, sliced
1 oz (25g) capers

•

NUTRITION PROFILE

*This low-calorie, low-fat soup is a good
source of Vitamin C and folic acid.*

• Per portion •
Carbohydrate: 6.6g
Protein: 1.6g Fibre: 2.8g
Fat: 0.5g Calories: 35

*The combination of the spices and the garnish give this low-calorie soup
a delicious tang. Serve with crusty (see p. 64) or herb bread and, if you
are not watching your calorie or fat intake, add a swirl of sour cream.*

Preparation time: 25 mins   Cooking time: 30 mins
Serves 4

METHOD

1. Put the beetroot, turnips and stock in a saucepan. Bring to the
boil and simmer for 15–20 minutes until the beetroot and turnips
are tender. Cool slightly.

2. Purée in a blender or food processor until smooth. Return to a
clean saucepan and bring to the boil. Add the thyme, bouquet
garni, mustard, horseradish, lemon juice and yeast extract and
simmer for 5 minutes.

3. Dissolve the arrowroot in 2 tsp (10ml) water and add the
mixture to the soup. Bring to the boil and simmer for 2–3
minutes, stirring. Season to taste.

4. Serve hot with lightly fried red onion slices and a few capers.

Illustrated on page 41

CELERIAC SOUP
WITH LEMON AND LOVAGE

INGREDIENTS

¼ onion, peeled and chopped
1 lb (500g) celeriac, chopped
rind of ½ lemon
½ tsp ground white mustard seeds
2 fl oz (50ml) dry white wine
1¼ pints (750ml) light stock or water
juice of ½ lemon
1 tsp (5ml) finely chopped fresh lovage

•

NUTRITION PROFILE

*This is low in fat and calories and contains
a useful amount of iron and Vitamin C.*

• Per portion •
Carbohydrate: 3.4g
Protein: 2.2g Fibre: 6.2g
Fat: 0.2g Calories: 30

Add the lovage just before serving, or its flavour may be too strong.

Preparation time: 15 mins   Cooking time: 35 mins
Serves 4

METHOD

1. Put the onion, celeriac, lemon rind, mustard seed, white wine
and stock in a medium saucepan.

2. Bring to the boil and simmer for about 30 minutes. Purée in a
blender or food processor until just smooth.

3. Pour the soup into a clean saucepan and add the lemon juice,
chopped lovage and seasoning. Simmer for 2 minutes. Serve hot,
garnished with sprigs of lovage and a sprinkling of lemon rind.

Illustrated on page 41

From top: **Soup Chinese style** (*see p. 37*); **Miso soup with arame and broccoli** (*see p. 36*);
Lettuce and sorrel soup with peppermint (*see p. 37*).

SPINACH ～ BROCCOLI SOUP WITH TARRAGON

INGREDIENTS

1 lb (500g) broccoli, roughly chopped
8oz (250g) spinach, roughly chopped
1 pint (600ml) light stock or water
1 tsp (5ml) green peppercorns, crushed
2 tsp (10ml) yeast extract
2 tsp (10ml) chopped fresh tarragon
2 tbsp (30ml) chopped chives
salt and black pepper

GARNISH
2 tbsp (30ml) chopped chives or a few
steamed broccoli florets

•

NUTRITION PROFILE

*This low-calorie, high-fibre soup contains
very little fat and is rich in iron, calcium,
magnesium and Vitamins A, B_2, B_6, C,
E and folic acid.*

• Per portion •
Carbohydrate: 4g
Protein: 8.3g **Fibre:** 8.5g
Fat: 0.3g **Calories:** 50

*Packed with vitamins and minerals, this soup makes a healthy start to a
meal at any time of year. When fresh spinach is not available, use
frozen and, if necessary, substitute calabrese for broccoli. For a splash
of contrasting colour, serve with a swirl of natural yogurt.*

Preparation time: 20 mins   Cooking time: 15 mins
Serves 4

METHOD

1. Put the broccoli, spinach and stock in a large saucepan. Bring
to the boil and simmer for 10 minutes or until the vegetables are
tender. Leave to cool.

2. Purée in a blender or food processor for a few seconds and
reheat gently.

3. Add the peppercorns to the soup with the yeast extract,
tarragon and chives. Season to taste.

4. Simmer for a further 2–3 minutes. Garnish with chives or
lightly steamed broccoli florets.

Illustrated opposite

FRESH GARLIC SOUP WITH ROSEMARY

INGREDIENTS

4 large cloves garlic, finely chopped (or
6–8 cloves dried garlic)
6oz (175g) potatoes, peeled and cubed
2 bay leaves
1½ tsp (7.5ml) chopped fresh
rosemary or savory
1 pint (600ml) semi-skimmed milk
salt and white pepper

•

NUTRITION PROFILE

*This soup is rich in calcium and
Vitamins B_2, B_{12} and C.*

• Per portion •
Carbohydrate: 18.6g
Protein: 5.6g **Fibre:** 1.1g
Fat: 5.1g **Calories:** 140

*This distinctively flavoured soup has a lovely white colour and a thin
texture. Served with garlic bread (see p.64) before a light meal, it
makes quite a filling starter. Garnish with rosemary.*

Preparation time: 15 mins   Cooking time: 20 mins
Serves 4

METHOD

1. Place the garlic in a saucepan together with the potatoes, bay
leaves, rosemary and milk.

2. Bring to the boil and simmer for 20 minutes or until the
potatoes are cooked. Remove the bay leaves.

3. Purée the soup in a blender or food processor until smooth.

4. Return the soup to a clean pan, reheat and adjust the
seasoning. Serve hot.

Illustrated opposite

Clockwise from top: **Beetroot and turnip soup with horseradish** (*see p.39*); **Fresh garlic soup with rosemary** (*see above*);
Spinach and broccoli soup with tarragon (*see above*); **Celeriac soup with lemon and lovage** (*see p.39*).

CAULIFLOWER AND CORIANDER SOUP

INGREDIENTS

1 cauliflower
$^{1}/_{2}$oz (15g) butter or margarine
1 onion, peeled and finely chopped
1 tsp (5ml) celery seeds
1 tsp (5ml) ground coriander
2 bay leaves
1 bouquet garni
1$^{1}/_{2}$ pints (900ml) light stock or water
$^{1}/_{2}$ tsp Dijon mustard
salt and black pepper

•

NUTRITION PROFILE

*This low-calorie soup is a good source of
Vitamin C.*

• Per portion •
Carbohydrate: 3.5g
Protein: 2.8g   **Fibre:** 1.3g
Fat: 3.3g   **Calories:** 55

*This creamy soup tastes best if you use a fresh and tender cauliflower
and serve it as soon as it is ready. If the cauliflower is hard, blanch it in
water for 3 minutes before use to remove the bitterness. For an
attractive garnish, steam a few florets for 5 minutes until tender and
add them to the soup immediately before serving.*

Preparation time: 15 mins   Cooking time: 35 mins
Serves 4

METHOD

1. Chop some of the cauliflower stalk and the florets into
small cubes.

2. Melt the butter in a large saucepan and gently fry the onion
and cubed cauliflower stalk, covered, for 5 minutes, without
letting them brown.

3. Add the celery seeds, coriander, bay leaves, bouquet garni and
a pinch of salt. Cook for a further 5 minutes, stirring occasionally.

4. Add the chopped florets and stock, bring to the boil and
simmer for 20 minutes. Remove the bay leaves and bouquet garni.
Cool slightly.

5. Purée in a blender or food processor for a few seconds until
creamy. Reheat in a clean saucepan. Stir in the mustard and
seasoning and simmer for 2–3 minutes. Serve as soon as possible.

Illustrated on page 44

QUICK TOFU ~ TOMATO SOUP

INGREDIENTS

1 large red pepper
1 lb (500g) tomatoes
5oz (150g) silken tofu
¼ tsp Tabasco sauce
pinch salt

GARNISH
chopped fresh parsley
•

NUTRITION PROFILE

Low in calories and fat and rich in Vitamins A, C and E, this soup is also high in copper and calcium.

• Per portion •
Carbohydrate: 4.6g
Protein: 3.3g **Fibre:** 2.2g
Fat: 1.2g **Calories:** 45

Silken tofu is an ideal low-fat base for a smooth soup. It becomes wonderfully creamy when blended, enhances the predominating flavour of the other ingredients, and adds protein to the dish.

Preparation time: 20 mins (plus chilling time)
Serves 4

METHOD

1. Blanch the pepper in boiling water for 10–15 minutes or until the skin comes off easily. Deseed and chop. Blanch the tomatoes in boiling water for 1–2 minutes. Skin and chop.

2. Purée the peppers and tomatoes with all the other ingredients in a blender or food processor until smooth. Chill.

3. If the soup begins to "set", process for a few seconds just before serving. Garnish with chopped fresh parsley.

Illustrated on page 44

LEEK ~ POTATO SOUP

INGREDIENTS

½oz (15g) butter or margarine
4oz (125g) shallots or 1 small onion, peeled and chopped
1 lb (500g) leeks, chopped
8oz (250g) potatoes, scrubbed and diced
1 bouquet garni
1 pint (600ml) stock or water
¼ pint (150ml) dry white wine
1 vegetable stock cube
2 tsp (10ml) lemon juice
½ tsp grated nutmeg
4 tbsp (60ml) chopped fresh parsley

GARNISH
1 tbsp (15ml) chopped fresh chives
•

NUTRITION PROFILE

This low-fat, high-fibre soup is a good source of calcium and Vitamins B$_6$ and C.

• Per portion •
Carbohydrate: 23.3g
Protein: 4.4g **Fibre:** 6.3g
Fat: 3.2g **Calories:** 150

This dry, white, warming soup is good on cold autumn evenings. The wine helps to lighten the flavour of the sweet vegetables. Clean the leeks carefully before use to remove any grit.

Preparation time: 20 mins   Cooking time: 35 mins
Serves 4

METHOD

1. Melt the butter in a saucepan and gently fry the shallots for 1–2 minutes. Add the leeks and potatoes and fry for another 2–3 minutes.

2. Add the bouquet garni, stock, white wine and stock cube. Bring to the boil and simmer for 25 minutes or until the potatoes are cooked. Cool slightly and remove the bouquet garni.

3. Purée in a blender or food processor until smooth.

4. Reheat gently in a clean saucepan with the lemon juice, nutmeg and chopped parsley. Bring to the boil and simmer for 1–2 minutes. Garnish with chives and serve with grated cheese.

Illustrated on page 44

FENNEL SOUP WITH ANISEED

INGREDIENTS

10–12oz (300–375g) fennel bulb
2 tsp (10ml) butter or margarine
1 medium onion, peeled and chopped
1 tsp (5ml) aniseeds
1 bay leaf
2 sticks celery, trimmed and chopped
1¼ pints (750ml) water
salt and white pepper

GARNISH
chopped fennel leaves

•

NUTRITION PROFILE

*This low-calorie soup is a good source of
Vitamin C.*

• Per portion •
Carbohydrate: 4.5g
Protein: 2.4g **Fibre:** 4.2g
Fat: 3.3g **Calories:** 55

*Aniseed, fennel and celery have complementary flavours and textures
and in this recipe are combined to make a light, fresh-tasting starter.
Try to find a fennel bulb that still has its leaves, to use as a garnish.*

Preparation time: 10 mins   Cooking time: 35 mins
Serves 4

METHOD

1. Cut off the feathery tops from the fennel and remove any
damaged outside stalks. Wash the bulb and drain. Cut off the
hard base, cut into quarters lengthwise and then chop across.

2. Melt the butter or margarine in a saucepan and gently fry the
onion. Add the aniseeds and bay leaf and cook for 5 minutes. Stir
in the fennel and celery and cook for a further 10 minutes.

3. Pour in the water, bring to the boil and simmer for 15 minutes
in a covered pan. Remove the bay leaf. Leave to cool. In a
blender or food processor, purée until smooth.

4. Reheat, season, garnish and serve hot.

Illustrated opposite

CREAMED ARTICHOKE SOUP

INGREDIENTS

12oz (375g) Jerusalem artichokes
1 tsp (5ml) vegetable margarine or
sunflower oil
1 small onion, peeled and chopped
4 sticks celery, trimmed and chopped
2 tsp (10ml) grated fresh root ginger
1½ pints (900ml) light stock
1 bouquet garni

GARNISH
4 small gherkins, chopped or sliced

•

NUTRITION PROFILE

*This low-fat, low-calorie soup contains a
useful amount of Vitamin E.*

• Per portion •
Carbohydrate: 3.7g
Protein: 1.8g **Fibre:** 0.6g
Fat: 1.3g **Calories:** 35

*Jerusalem artichokes are rather time-consuming to peel but have a nutty
flavour which goes well with ginger.*

Preparation time: 20 mins   Cooking time: 30 mins
Serves 4

METHOD

1. Peel and chop the artichokes.

2. Melt the margarine in a saucepan and gently cook the onion,
celery, ginger and Jerusalem artichokes for 1–2 minutes.

3. Add the stock and bouquet garni. Cover and simmer for
20–25 minutes or until the Jerusalem artichokes are tender.
Allow to cool slightly. Remove the bouquet garni.

4. Purée in a blender or food processor until smooth. Pour the
soup into a clean saucepan, season and reheat. Serve hot,
garnished with the gherkins.

Illustrated on page 47

Clockwise from top left: **Leek and potato soup** (*see p.43*); **Quick tofu and tomato soup** (*see p.43*);
Cauliflower and coriander soup (*see p.42*); **Fennel soup with aniseed** (*see above*).

KOHLRABI ~~ WATERCRESS SOUP

INGREDIENTS

14oz (450g) green kohlrabi
1½ pints (900ml) light stock or water
3oz (75g) celery, trimmed and chopped
½ tsp fresh green chilli, deseeded
and chopped
1oz (25g) green pepper, deseeded
and chopped
1oz (25g) watercress, chopped
2 tsp (10ml) chopped fresh sage
large pinch grated nutmeg
salt and black pepper

•

NUTRITION PROFILE

*This low-calorie, low-fat soup is also a rich
source of Vitamin C and folic acid.*

• Per portion •
Carbohydrate: 6.3g
Protein: 2.3g   Fibre: 1.8g
Fat: 0.2g   Calories: 35

◆

*This is an extremely healthy starter – full of Vitamin C and very low in
calories and fat. The combination of watercress, chilli and peppers gives
the soup a good strong, spicy flavour.*

Preparation time: 20 mins   Cooking time: 45 mins
Serves 4

METHOD

1. Peel the kohlrabi, reserving the leaves to use as a garnish.

2. Put the stock in a large saucepan and bring to the boil. Add the
kohlrabi and celery and simmer for 40 minutes.

3. Add the chilli, green pepper and watercress. Cook for a further
5 minutes. Leave to cool.

4. In a blender or food processor, purée until smooth. Transfer to
a clean saucepan. Add the sage and nutmeg and season to taste.
Reheat gently.

5. Meanwhile, steam the kohlrabi leaves until tender then chop
and use to garnish the soup.

Illustrated opposite

EASY PUMPKIN SOUP

INGREDIENTS

2 lb (1kg) ripe orange pumpkin, outer
skin and non-orange parts removed
4 fl oz (125ml) water
1½ pints (900ml) semi-skimmed milk
salt and white pepper
1 tsp (5ml) honey (optional)

•

NUTRITION PROFILE

*This calcium-rich soup is also high in
Vitamins A, B_1, B_2, B_{12} and C.*

• Per portion •
Carbohydrate: 19.8g
Protein: 9.4g   Fibre: 1.3g
Fat: 3.8g   Calories: 145

*Served with thick slices of wholemeal bread, this soup makes a delicious
and satisfying supper dish on a cold evening.*

Preparation time: 10 mins   Cooking time: 30 mins
Serves 4

METHOD

1. Scoop out the pumpkin and set the seeds on one side. Dice the
orange pumpkin flesh and put in a saucepan with the water.
Simmer for about 15 minutes until soft.

2. Mash until smooth. Add the milk, bring to the boil and
simmer for 5 minutes. Season to taste and add honey if liked.

3. Meanwhile, wash and toast the pumpkin seeds in a preheated
oven at Gas Mark 5, 375°F, 190°C until crisp and brown. Serve
the soup with croûtons (see p.67) or crusty bread (see p.64) and
pumpkin seeds as a side snack.

Illustrated opposite

From top: **Creamed artichoke soup** (*see p.45*); **Easy pumpkin soup** (*see above*); **Kohlrabi and watercress soup** (*see above*).

CHEESE ~AND~ PARSNIP SOUP
WITH CARAWAY

INGREDIENTS

½oz (15g) butter or margarine
1 small onion, peeled and chopped
1 tsp (5ml) caraway seeds
3oz (75g) fennel, chopped
2oz (50g) potatoes, scrubbed and diced
10oz (300g) parsnips, cubed
1¼ pints (750ml) stock or water
2oz (50g) Cheddar cheese, grated

•

NUTRITION PROFILE

This soup contains some Vitamin B_{12} and is a good source of folic acid, calcium and Vitamin C.

• Per portion •
Carbohydrate: 13.5g
Protein: 7.4g **Fibre:** 4.6g
Fat: 9.6g **Calories:** 165

Choose small or medium parsnips, avoiding any with dark patches.

Preparation time: 20 mins   Cooking time: 30 mins
Serves 4

METHOD

1. Heat the butter in a saucepan and gently fry the onion with the caraway seeds until the onion is soft. Add the fennel and potatoes, and fry for a further 2–3 minutes.

2. Add the parsnips to the pan and fry for 1–2 minutes. Stir in the stock, bring to the boil, cover and simmer for 20–25 minutes. Cool slightly. Purée in a blender or food processor until smooth.

3. Reheat gently in a clean saucepan and bring to boiling point. Add the grated cheese and seasoning, stirring until the cheese has melted. Garnish with caraway seeds or cheese, and serve hot.

Illustrated opposite

GREEN SPLIT PEA SOUP
WITH CORIANDER

INGREDIENTS

1 tbsp (15ml) sunflower oil
1 onion, peeled and chopped
1 tsp (5ml) coriander seeds
1 clove garlic, crushed
2 sticks celery, trimmed and chopped
8oz (250g) green split peas
1½ pints (900ml) light stock or water
6oz (175g) mangetout peas
½oz (15g) coarsely chopped fresh coriander
2 tsp (10ml) shoyu or tamari
salt and black pepper

•

NUTRITION PROFILE

This low-fat, high-protein, high-fibre soup is rich in Vitamins B_1, C and E and in magnesium, iron and zinc.

• Per portion •
Carbohydrate: 41g
Protein: 16g **Fibre:** 8.4g
Fat: 4.7g **Calories:** 265

This satisfying winter soup has a strong flavour of fresh coriander. Coriander quickly loses its flavour in water, so do not boil the soup after adding it. Shoyu or tamari also adds extra flavour.

Preparation time: 25 mins
Cooking time: about 1 hour
Serves 4

METHOD

1. Heat the oil in a heavy-based saucepan and fry the onion and the coriander seeds until the onion is soft. Add the garlic and celery and fry for a further 5 minutes.

2. Rinse the split peas. Add to the pan and cook over a low heat for 2–3 minutes, stirring all the time. Pour in the stock, bring to the boil and simmer for 40 minutes or until the peas start disintegrating. At this point, add the mangetout peas and cook for a further 15 minutes.

3. Stir in the coriander, shoyu and seasoning. Reheat gently, but do not boil. Serve immediately.

Illustrated opposite

Clockwise from top: **Cheese and parsnip soup with caraway** (*see above*); **Green split pea soup with coriander** (*see above*); **Almond and tomato soup** (*see p. 50*).

CURRIED SOYA BEAN SOUP

INGREDIENTS

2oz (50g) soya beans, soaked
1¼ pints (750ml) water
1 tbsp (15ml) sunflower oil
1 medium onion, peeled and chopped
2 tsp (10ml) garam masala
6 curry leaves, chopped
2 bay leaves
2 sticks celery, chopped
1 medium carrot, scrubbed and diced
1 lb (500g) marrow, peeled, deseeded
and cubed
2 large tomatoes, skinned and diced
1 vegetable stock cube
2oz (50g) sultanas
salt and black pepper
•

NUTRITION PROFILE

This high-fibre soup is a good source of
magnesium, calcium, and Vitamins A,
C and E.

• Per portion •
Carbohydrate: 20.5g
Protein: 5.9g **Fibre:** 5.3g
Fat: 6g **Calories:** 155

Soya beans are the most nutritious beans of all. They contain all the
essential amino acids and help to make a substantial base for a soup.

Preparation time: 25 mins (plus 12 hours' minimum soaking)
Cooking time: 1 hour (plus 1–2 hours' for the soya beans)
Serves 4

METHOD

1. Drain the soya beans. Place in a saucepan with 1¼ pints (750ml) fresh water and simmer for 1–2 hours until soft.

2. Heat 2 tsp (10ml) of the oil in a saucepan and fry the onion. Add half the garam masala, curry leaves, bay leaves, celery and carrot. Cook for 5–10 minutes. Stir in the marrow, drained soya beans and tomatoes and cook for a further 2–3 minutes.

3. Make up the reserved cooking water to 1¼ pints (750ml) and add it to the saucepan. Crumble the vegetable stock cube into the saucepan and add the sultanas. Cook for 45 minutes.

4. Gently heat the remaining oil in a small pan and fry the rest of the garam masala for 1–2 minutes, until a spicy aroma rises. Add to the soup and cook for another 5 minutes. Season and serve hot.

Illustrated on page 52

ALMOND AND TOMATO SOUP

INGREDIENTS

1 pint (600ml) water
6 large ripe tomatoes, chopped
2 bay leaves
2 tsp (10ml) paprika
4oz (125g) almonds, blanched

GARNISH
toasted flaked almonds
•

NUTRITION PROFILE

This soup is rich in iron, zinc, magnesium,
calcium, folic acid, Vitamins A, B_2,
C and E.

• Per portion •
Carbohydrate: 4.9g
Protein: 6.1g **Fibre:** 5.6g
Fat: 15.7g **Calories:** 185

This orange-pink soup makes a colourful display on a dinner table.

Preparation time: 30 mins Cooking time: 20 mins
Serves 4

METHOD

1. Simmer the water, tomatoes and bay leaves for 15 minutes. Add the paprika and cook for 5 minutes. Leave to cool.

2. Meanwhile, toast the almonds under a preheated grill until golden on both sides. Allow them to cool and then grind to a very fine powder or paste in a coffee grinder or food processor.

3. Purée the tomato mixture and the almonds together in a blender or food processor until smooth. Pour into a clean saucepan and reheat without boiling. Serve hot.

Illustrated on page 49

SPICED LENTIL SOUP WITH COCONUT

INGREDIENTS

1 tbsp (15ml) sunflower oil
2 medium onions, peeled and chopped
1 clove garlic, crushed
1 bay leaf
1 tsp (5ml) grated fresh root ginger
2 tsp (10ml) turmeric
$\frac{1}{2}$ tsp cumin seeds, crushed
$\frac{1}{2}$ tsp coriander seeds, crushed
1 tsp (5ml) white mustard seeds,
crushed
8oz (250g) red split lentils
$1\frac{1}{2}$ pints (900ml) water
1oz (25g) creamed coconut, grated
1 tsp (5ml) lemon juice
salt and black pepper

GARNISH
4 slices of lemon, cut into twists

•

NUTRITION PROFILE

This soup is high in protein and fibre, and a good source of Vitamins B_6, B_{12}, C and E, iron and zinc.

• Per portion •
Carbohydrate: 35.1g
Protein: 14.8g **Fibre:** 8.3g
Fat: 7.8g **Calories:** 260

A variation on a Middle Eastern recipe, this soup derives nutritional value from the lentils, which are a good, cheap source of protein and fibre and do not need soaking before cooking. The spices give the dish an attractive appearance and a slightly hot taste. For the best flavour, grind your own spices in a food processor or a small electric grinder.

Preparation time: 20 mins   Cooking time: 20 mins
Serves 4

METHOD

1. Heat the oil in a large saucepan and gently fry the onion, covered, until soft. Add the garlic, bay leaf, half the grated ginger, the turmeric, cumin, coriander and mustard seeds. Fry for a further 1–2 minutes.

2. Add the red split lentils and cook for 1 minute, stirring. Pour in the water, bring to the boil and simmer for 15 minutes.

3. Give the soup a good stir, add the rest of the grated ginger and cook for another 5 minutes.

4. Stir in the coconut, lemon juice and seasoning.

5. When the coconut is dissolved, bring up to boiling point, then remove the bay leaf. Serve hot, garnish with twists of lemon.

Illustrated on page 52

MANY BEAN SOUP

INGREDIENTS

1oz (25g) red kidney beans
1oz (25g) aduki beans
1oz (25g) mung beans
1oz (25g) pinto beans
1oz (25g) black-eye beans
1oz (25g) flageolet beans
1 tbsp (15ml) sunflower oil
1 onion, peeled and chopped
½ tsp caraway seeds
¼ tsp cardamom seeds, lightly crushed
¼ tsp aniseeds, lightly crushed
1 carrot, scrubbed and sliced
6oz (175g) leeks, chopped
2 tsp (10ml) chopped fresh mint

•

NUTRITION PROFILE

This soup is rich in magnesium, calcium, iron, Vitamins A, B₁, C and E, and fibre.

• Per portion •
Carbohydrate: 22.2g
Protein: 9.6g **Fibre:** 8.3g
Fat: 4.4g **Calories:** 165

Made with six different pulses, this soup has an instant appeal. Caraway and aniseeds bring a nice, sharp flavour to the dish.

Preparation time: 20 mins (plus 12 hours' minimum soaking)
Cooking time: 1½ hours
Serves 4

METHOD

1. Drain the beans and place in a saucepan with plenty of fresh water. Boil fast for 10 minutes, then simmer for about 50 minutes.

2. Heat the oil in a medium saucepan and fry the onion until soft. Add all the seeds and cook for 1–2 minutes. Stir in the carrot and leeks and fry until the leek has softened.

3. Drain the cooked beans, reserving 2 pints (1.2 litres) of the stock. Add the beans and stock to the saucepan and cook for 25 minutes or until the stock has thickened.

4. Stir in the mint and a little lemon juice and cook for another 2–3 minutes. Season and serve hot.

Illustrated opposite

BROWN LENTIL ᴬᴺᴰ MUSHROOM SOUP

INGREDIENTS

1 tbsp (15ml) sunflower or olive oil
1 onion, peeled and finely chopped
2 cloves garlic, crushed
8 oz (250g) mushrooms, chopped
8oz (250g) brown lentils
2 tsp (10ml) fresh savory
2 tsp (10ml) fresh chervil
1¾ pints (1 litre) dark stock or water
1 tsp (5ml) yeast extract
1 tbsp (15ml) chopped fresh parsley

•

NUTRITION PROFILE

This high-protein, high-fibre soup is rich in Vitamins B₁, B₂, C and E, iron, zinc, copper, magnesium, niacin and folic acid.

• Per portion •
Carbohydrate: 35.2g
Protein: 17g **Fibre:** 9.4g
Fat: 4.8g **Calories:** 245

This is a warming, filling soup on a cold evening, and when served with crusty or garlic bread (see p. 64) can make a complete meal. Lentils are an excellent source of protein and give the soup substance.

Preparation time: 20 mins Cooking time: 1 hour
Serves 4

METHOD

1. Heat the oil in a heavy-based saucepan and fry the onion and garlic until tender. Add the mushrooms and fry for a further 5 minutes. Add the lentils and herbs. Stir the ingredients for another 2–3 minutes.

2. Mix in the stock and yeast extract, bring to the boil and simmer for 50 minutes.

3. Season to taste and sprinkle on the chopped parsley. Simmer for another 2–3 minutes and serve.

Illustrated opposite

Clockwise from top left: **Curried soya bean soup** (*see p. 50*); **Spiced lentil soup with coconut** (*see p. 51*); **Brown lentil and mushroom soup** (*see above*); **Many bean soup** (*see above*); **Sweet potato and avocado soup** (*see p. 54*).

SWEET POTATO ~ AVOCADO SOUP

INGREDIENTS

1 lb (500g) sweet potatoes, scrubbed
1½ pints (900ml) water
1 small onion, peeled and
finely chopped
1 ripe avocado, peeled and stoned
grated rind and juice of ½ lemon
grated rind and juice of 1 large orange
½ tsp ground mace
pinch salt

GARNISH
few avocado slices

•

NUTRITION PROFILE

*This soup is rich in folic acid and Vitamins
A, B₁, B₆, C and E.*

• Per portion •
Carbohydrate: 29.7g
Protein: 3.7g **Fibre:** 4.4g
Fat: 11.3g **Calories:** 230

*There are many varieties of sweet potato, with flesh ranging from
nearly white to magenta or purple. The colour of the soup will be
determined by the type of potato. You could use yams instead.*

Preparation time: 15 mins   Cooking time: 20 mins
Serves 4

METHOD

1. Cut any woody parts off the sweet potatoes. Peel and dice.

2. Bring the water to the boil in a saucepan, add the potatoes and
onion and simmer for about 15 minutes. Cool slightly.

3. Mix the avocado flesh and potato mixture in a blender or food
processor until smooth. Reheat the soup in a clean saucepan,
adding the rind and juice of the lemon and orange, the mace and
a pinch of salt. Simmer for 1–2 minutes.

4. Garnish with avocado slices and serve immediately.

Illustrated on page 52

MARMITE BOUCHERONNE

INGREDIENTS

4oz (125g) butter beans, soaked
4oz (125g) dried chestnuts, soaked in
1½ pints (900ml) water
1 tbsp (15ml) sunflower oil
1 onion, peeled and chopped
6 whole cloves
2 bay leaves
8oz (250g) carrots, scrubbed and cubed
12oz (375g) Brussels sprouts, trimmed
1½ pints (900ml) stock or water
1 tbsp (15ml) miso

•

NUTRITION PROFILE

*This soup is high in fibre and protein, low
in fat and rich in Vitamins A, B₁, B₆, C
and E, folic acid, calcium, magnesium,
iron, copper and fibre.*

• Per portion •
Carbohydrate: 35.1g
Protein: 10.8g **Fibre:** 12.6g
Fat: 5g **Calories:** 220

*"Marmite" is a French term for a type of stew or broth. It is also the
name of the large, earthenware pot in which it is traditionally made.*

Preparation time: 25 mins (plus 12 hours' minimum soaking)
Cooking time: 1½ hours
Serves 4

METHOD

1. Drain the butter beans and place in a saucepan with the
chestnuts and their soaking water. Cook for about 40–50 minutes
until both are tender. Drain and reserve the stock.

2. Heat the oil in a large saucepan and fry the onion until soft.
Add the cloves, bay leaves, carrots and sprouts and stir for 3–5
minutes. Make up the cooking water from the beans and
chestnuts to 1½ pints (900ml) and add to the pan.

3. Bring to the boil, add the beans and cooked chestnuts and
simmer for 30 minutes. Season and cook for another 2–3
minutes. Remove from the heat, add the miso and stir. Serve hot.

Illustrated on page 56

MUSHROOM SOUP WITH A PASTRY LID

INGREDIENTS

1oz (25g) butter or margarine
1 onion, peeled and chopped
12oz (375g) oyster mushrooms,
chopped
1 tbsp (15ml) fresh dill, chopped
1 pint (600ml) dark stock (see p.30)
1 tsp (5ml) yeast extract
2 tsp (10ml) medium-dry sherry
salt and black pepper

PASTRY

6oz (175g) wholemeal plain flour
pinch salt
1 tsp (5ml) dill seeds
3oz (75g) butter or margarine
2 tsp (10ml) sunflower oil
2–3 tbsp (30–45ml) water

GLAZE

beaten egg

•

NUTRITION PROFILE

*This high-fibre starter is rich in Vitamins
A, B$_1$, B$_2$, C and E, niacin, magnesium,
iron, copper and folic acid.*

• Per portion •
Carbohydrate: 30.6g
Protein: 8.5g **Fibre:** 6.9g
Fat: 24.7g **Calories:** 375

*The "pastry lid" on each individual bowl makes a delicious and
substantial garnish. Decorate the lid with leaves made from any leftover
pastry, or else with a sprig of parsley.*

Preparation time: 40 mins (plus 10 mins resting time for the dough)
Cooking time: 20–25 mins
Serves 4

METHOD

1. Melt the butter in a saucepan and fry the onions for 2–3
minutes. Add the mushrooms and dill and fry for a further 5
minutes. Stir in the stock, yeast extract and sherry. Cook for a
further 10 minutes or until the mushrooms are tender. Season to
taste and leave to cool. Purée in a blender or food processor for a
few seconds. Pour into 4 ovenproof soup bowls.

2. For the pastry, mix the flour with the salt and dill seeds. Rub in
the butter until the mixture resembles breadcrumbs.

3. Mix the oil and water together and add two-thirds to the flour
mixture. Form into a medium-soft dough, adding the remaining
oil and water if necessary. Leave the dough to rest for 10 minutes.

4. Prepare the pastry lids (see below). Glaze with beaten egg.
Bake in a preheated oven at Gas Mark 6, 400°F, 200°C for 20–25
minutes or until the pastry is golden brown and crisp. Serve hot.

Illustrated on page 56

MAKING A PASTRY LID

*Pastry, not known for its nutritional qualities, can nevertheless be made healthier by using less fat, switching
from refined flour to wholemeal flour, or by making an egg-free variety. A pastry lid on a warming soup can
provide the carbohydrate and protein necessary for a well-balanced meal.*

1. Take a quarter of the pastry and roll
into 4 thin strips. Dampen the rims and
press a strip onto each.

2. Divide the rest of the pastry into 4,
and roll out each quarter fairly thickly
to form a 'lid'.

3. Dampen the pastry rims and place
the lids on top of the serving bowls.
Press down the sides to seal.

COURGETTE ^{AND} WALNUT SOUP

INGREDIENTS

1 tbsp (15ml) olive oil
1 small onion, peeled and chopped
1 tsp (5ml) cumin
pinch chilli powder
8oz (250g) courgettes, diced
2oz (50g) button mushrooms, thickly
sliced or quartered
2oz (50g) whole oats
2oz (50g) shelled walnuts, chopped
1¼ pints (750ml) stock or water
2 tsp (10ml) fresh marjoram
2 tbsp (30ml) tahini
1 tsp (5ml) lemon juice

•

NUTRITION PROFILE

*This soup is a good source of iron, zinc,
magnesium, and Vitamins B₁ and C.*

• Per portion •
Carbohydrate: 14.8g
Protein: 6.8g **Fibre:** 3.5g
Fat: 16.7g **Calories:** 230

*This delicious protein-rich soup is thickened and enriched with tahini, a
sesame seed paste. Take care not to boil the soup after the tahini is
added or it may curdle and separate. Choose small, firm courgettes, no
longer than 6 inches (15cm) in length.*

Preparation time: 20 mins   Cooking time: 35 mins
Serves 4

METHOD

1. Heat the oil in a saucepan and gently fry the onion until soft.
Add the cumin and chilli powder and cook over a low heat for
1–2 minutes.

2. Stir in the courgettes, mushrooms, oats and walnuts and cook
over a medium heat for 3–4 minutes. When the courgettes turn
golden, add the stock, bring to the boil and simmer for 20–25
minutes or until the oats are cooked.

3. Add the marjoram, season and cook for a further 2–3 minutes.
Remove from the heat, stir in the tahini and lemon juice.

Illustrated opposite

GREEK FASSOLADA

INGREDIENTS

6oz (175g) haricot beans, soaked
1 tbsp (15ml) olive oil
1 large onion, peeled and chopped
2 medium carrots, scrubbed and sliced
2 cloves garlic, crushed
2 sticks celery, trimmed and chopped
8oz (250g) potatoes, peeled
and chopped
4 tomatoes, skinned and chopped
20 black olives, stoned

•

NUTRITION PROFILE

*This high-protein, high-fibre starter is rich
in magnesium, iron, calcium, copper,
zinc, Vitamins A, B₁, B₆, C and E.*

• Per portion •
Carbohydrate: 37.4g
Protein: 12.1g **Fibre:** 15.4g
Fat: 6.2g **Calories:** 250

*This satisfying, yet low-fat and inexpensive soup is a smooth version of
one of the national dishes of Greece.*

Preparation time: 20 mins (plus 12 hours' minimum soaking)
Cooking time: 1½–2 hours
Serves 4

METHOD

1. Drain the haricot beans. Place in a saucepan of fresh water and
simmer for about 1 hour. Purée half of the beans with 1¼ pints
(750ml) of their cooking water in a blender or food processor.

2. Heat the oil in a saucepan and fry the onion and carrot until
soft. Add the garlic and celery and fry for a further 2–3 minutes.
Add the potatoes, tomatoes, puréed beans and the remaining
whole beans and cook for 25–30 minutes.

3. Stir in the olives and 2 tsp (10ml) chopped fresh parsley. Cook
for 2–3 minutes and season to taste. Serve hot.

Illustrated on page 59

From top: **Marmite boucheronne** (*see p.54*); Courgette and walnut soup (*see above*);
Mushroom soup with a pastry lid (*see p.55*).

SCOTTISH COUNTRY SOUP

INGREDIENTS

1 tbsp (15ml) sunflower oil
1 medium onion, chopped
6oz (175g) carrots, scrubbed and diced
4oz (125g) leeks, chopped
4oz (125g) fresh or frozen peas
4oz (125g) winter cabbage, chopped
2oz (50g) barley flakes
1 bouquet garni
1 tsp (5ml) fresh marjoram
1 tsp (5ml) fresh thyme
2 pints (1.2 litres) semi-skimmed milk

•

NUTRITION PROFILE

*This high-protein soup is rich in Vitamins
A, B_1, B_2, B_6, B_{12} and C, niacin, folic
acid, zinc, calcium and magnesium.*

• Per portion •
Carbohydrate: 35.4g
Protein: 15g **Fibre:** 6.1g
Fat: 9.2g **Calories:** 270

*Barley, which is particularly high in niacin, gives a substantial base to
this satisfying vegetable soup, while the milk adds protein and thickness.
Serve with dumplings (see p.63) for a really hearty soup.*

Preparation time: 20 mins   Cooking time: 50 mins
Serves 4

METHOD

1. Heat the oil in a large saucepan and gently fry the onion and
carrots for 5–10 minutes.

2. Add the leeks, peas and cabbage and cook for a further
1–2 minutes.

3. Stir in the barley flakes, bouquet garni, marjoram, thyme and
milk and cook for 30 minutes.

4. Season and cook for another 10 minutes, remove the bouquet
garni and serve.

Illustrated opposite

FARM SOUP WITH WHEAT BERRIES

INGREDIENTS

1 tbsp (15ml) sunflower oil
1 onion, peeled and finely chopped
2oz (50g) parsnips, peeled and diced
1 bay leaf
6oz (175g) small cauliflower florets
5oz (150g) runner beans, chopped
8oz (250g) red split lentils
1¾ pints (1 litre) light stock
1 tsp (5ml) fresh rosemary
1 tbsp (15ml) chopped fresh parsley
2oz (50g) wheat berries, cooked

•

NUTRITION PROFILE

*This low-fat soup is rich in fibre, protein,
iron, zinc, magnesium, folic acid and
Vitamins B_1, B_6 and C.*

• Per portion •
Carbohydrate: 47g
Protein: 18.9g **Fibre:** 12.3g
Fat: 1.2g **Calories:** 260

*Lentils always make for a good, hearty soup. This one is no exception.
It contains a mixture of grains, vegetables and pulses, and produces a
very filling soup.*

Preparation time: 45 mins (plus 40–50 mins for the wheat berries)
Cooking time: 20 mins
Serves 4

METHOD

1. Heat the oil in a large saucepan and fry the onion, parsnips and
bay leaf until the onion is soft.

2. Mix in the cauliflower florets and runner beans and cook for 5
minutes. Mix in the red split lentils, stock, rosemary and parsley
and cook for 15 minutes.

3. Stir the soup thoroughly and cook for 10 minutes. Add the
wheat berries and cook for a further 10 minutes. Remove the bay
leaf. Season to taste and serve.

Illustrated opposite

Clockwise from top: **Scottish country soup** (*see above*); **Greek fassolada** (*see p.57*); **Farm soup with wheat berries** (*see above*).

VEGETABLE SOUP WITH PESTO

INGREDIENTS

1½ tsp (7.5ml) olive oil
½ large onion, peeled and chopped
1–2 cloves garlic, crushed
1 tsp (5ml) fresh basil
½ red pepper, deseeded and chopped
4oz (125g) French beans
2oz (50g) wholemeal macaroni
1¼ pints (750ml) tomato
stock (see p.28)
1 vegetable stock cube
6–8oz (175–250g) cherry tomatoes

PESTO

1–2 cloves garlic, crushed
1oz (25g) grated Parmesan cheese
1oz (25g) toasted pine nuts, ground
2oz (50g) skimmed milk soft cheese
1½oz (40g) fresh basil

•

NUTRITION PROFILE

This soup is rich in Vitamin C and calcium.

• Per portion •
Carbohydrate: 16.3g
Protein: 8.8g   **Fibre:** 3.6g
Fat: 12.3g   **Calories:** 205

This low-fat version of pesto, a traditional Italian sauce, uses skimmed milk soft cheese instead of olive oil. The result is a delicious soup with a strong basil flavour. Use half the quantity of dried basil if you cannot get fresh. If cherry tomatoes are not available, use quartered tomatoes.

Preparation time: 30 mins   Cooking time: 35 mins
Serves 4

METHOD

1. Heat the oil in a large saucepan and fry the onion until transparent. Add the garlic and basil, cover and cook for a further 1–2 minutes.

2. Stir in the pepper, French beans and macaroni, coating them in the oil.

3. Add the stock and crumbled stock cube, bring to the boil and simmer for 15–20 minutes or until the macaroni and beans are cooked. Add the tomatoes and simmer for a further 5 minutes. Season to taste.

4. Prepare the pesto (see below). Pour the hot soup over the pesto, stir to melt the cheese and serve immediately.

Illustrated opposite

MAKING PESTO

Pesto is a traditional Italian sauce made from basil and garlic, originally from Genoa. It can be used as a sauce to accompany pasta or jacket potatoes or rice, and also works well as a base for soup. Garlic, a member of the onion family, is renowned for its benefits to the digestive system.

1. Crush 1–2 cloves garlic into a mixing bowl.

2. Mix with fresh basil, skimmed milk soft cheese, ground toasted pine nuts and Parmesan cheese to form a paste.

3. Place in a dish and pour hot soup over it. If using as a sauce, heat in a pan until the cheese melts, then serve.

From top: **Mexican gumbo** (*see p.62*); **Vegetable soup with pesto** (*see above*); **Cashew and sweetcorn chowder** (*see p.62*).

MEXICAN GUMBO

INGREDIENTS

3oz (75g) red kidney beans, soaked
1 tbsp (15ml) olive oil
1 onion, peeled and finely chopped
2 tsp (10ml) paprika
pinch chilli powder
1/8 tsp ground allspice
1 red pepper, deseeded and diced
1 green pepper, deseeded and diced
10oz (300g) sweet potatoes, scrubbed
4oz (125g) okra, chopped
1½ pints (900ml) stock or water
1 tbsp (15ml) tomato purée

•

NUTRITION PROFILE

*A good source of iron, copper, calcium,
magnesium and folic acid, this soup is also
rich in Vitamins A, B₁, B₆, C and E.*

• Per portion •
Carbohydrate: 34.5g
Protein: 9.6g **Fibre:** 11.6g
Fat: 5.2g **Calories:** 215

*This spicy, high-fibre soup derives its name from okra, also known as
gumbo. Use the bean water as stock, it will add flavour and minerals.*

Preparation time: 25 mins (plus 12 hours' minimum soaking)
Cooking time: 1 hour 40 mins
Serves 4

METHOD

1. Drain the beans. Place in a saucepan with plenty of fresh water
and boil fast for 10 minutes, then simmer for about 50 minutes
until tender. Drain and reserve the stock.

2. Heat the oil in a saucepan and gently fry the onion. Add the
spices and fry for 1–2 minutes, until a roasted aroma rises.

3. Stir in the peppers, cubed sweet potatoes and drained beans
and cook over a medium heat for 3–5 minutes. Add the okra and
the reserved stock. Bring to the boil and simmer for 30 minutes.

4. Stir in the tomato purée and seasoning and cook for a further 5
minutes. Serve hot.

Illustrated on page 61

CASHEW ᴬᴺᴰ SWEETCORN CHOWDER

INGREDIENTS

2 pints (1.2 litres) water
2 large corn cobs (or 6oz/175g
sweetcorn, frozen or canned)
1 vegetable stock cube
8oz (250g) unsalted cashew nuts
2 tbsp (30ml) wholemeal rice flour
½ onion, peeled and finely chopped
20 spring onions, trimmed and chopped
2 tbsp (30ml) chopped fresh parsley
salt and black pepper

•

NUTRITION PROFILE

*This soup is high in protein and fibre and is
a good source of calcium, magnesium, iron
and Vitamins B₁ and C.*

• Per portion •
Carbohydrate: 38.2g
Protein: 14.3g **Fibre:** 9.1g
Fat: 30.1g **Calories:** 465

*If using frozen or canned sweetcorn, you will only need 1³/4 pints
(1 litre) of water.*

Preparation time: 35 mins   Cooking time: 20 mins
Serves 4

METHOD

1. Simmer the corn cobs in the water for 12 minutes. Remove the
corn. Add the stock cube to the water and boil for 1–2 minutes.

2. Meanwhile, cut the kernels off the cob. Grind the cashew nuts
to a powder. Process half the ground nuts, half the rice flour and
half the cooled stock until smooth. Blend the remaining nuts,
flour and stock. Pour both into a pan.

3. Gently heat the soup, then add the onion, spring onions,
sweetcorn, parsley and seasoning to taste. Bring to the boil,
stirring continuously. Simmer for 5 minutes and serve hot.

Illustrated on page 61

ACCOMPANIMENTS

Savoury accompaniments and garnishes for both soups and starters are quick to prepare, but can immediately turn a light starter into a complete meal. Some can also be adapted and enlarged to make a nutritious snack. These recipes provide a useful basic selection and some ideas for improvisations to suit your own taste.

HERB DUMPLINGS

INGREDIENTS

2oz (50g) 85% wholemeal self-raising flour
pinch salt
$^{1}/_{2}$oz (15g) butter or margarine
1 egg, beaten
1 tbsp (15ml) skimmed milk
1 tbsp (15ml) chopped fresh herbs, such as parsley, dill, rosemary, sage or tarragon
black pepper

•

NUTRITION PROFILE

These contain a useful amount of Vitamins B_{12} and D.

• Per portion •
Carbohydrate: 8.8g
Protein: 3.4g **Fibre:** 1.2g
Fat: 4.4g **Calories:** 85

Dumplings can be flavoured by an infinite variety of herbs, so select a flavour complementary to the recipe. These dumplings turn a simple soup into a light lunch or a starter before a light main course. If you do not have wholemeal self-raising flour, use plain wholemeal and add $^{1}/_{2}$ tsp baking powder.

Preparation time: 15 mins   Cooking time: 10 mins
Serves 4

METHOD

1. Sift the flour with the salt into a bowl. Rub the butter into the flour.

2. Beat the egg with the milk and add the chopped herbs. Mix into the flour mixture and add a little black pepper. Leave to stand for 5 minutes.

3. Drop half-teaspoonfuls of the dough into the simmering soup. Simmer gently for 10 minutes. Turn the dumplings over halfway through the cooking time, so that they cook thoroughly.

Illustrated on page 65

CRUSTY BREAD

INGREDIENTS

2 tsp (10ml) butter or margarine
4 slices wholemeal bread

•

NUTRITION PROFILE

Bread is a good source of zinc, magnesium, Vitamin B_1 and niacin. Butter is rich in the fat-soluble Vitamins A, D and E.

• Per portion •
Carbohydrate: 10.5g
Protein: 2.2g **Fibre:** 2.1g
Fat: 2.7g **Calories:** 75

Warm, crusty bread is a great accompaniment to almost any hot or cold soup. This is a quick and easy way to make the best of stale bread, but the thicker the bread, the longer it will take to crisp up.

Preparation time: 5 mins Cooking time: 20 mins
Serves 4

METHOD

1. Butter the slices of bread and place on a baking sheet.

2. Crisp in a preheated oven at Gas Mark 5, 375°F, 190°C for 15–20 minutes.

3. Cool a little and serve while warm.

Illustrated opposite

GARLIC BREAD

INGREDIENTS

2 cloves garlic, crushed
4 tsp (20ml) butter or soft vegetable margarine
4 slices of bread or rounds of French bread

•

NUTRITION PROFILE

This contains useful amounts of calcium, iron, Vitamin A and B Vitamins.

• Per portion •
Carbohydrate: 11.8g
Protein: 2.2g **Fibre:** 0.7g
Fat: 4.5g **Calories:** 100

Excellent served with garlic-flavoured soups or with a pâté or spread, garlic bread is quick and easy to prepare. When buying garlic, choose plump and juicy cloves which will yield the best flavour when cooked.

Preparation time: 10 mins Cooking time: 15 mins
Serves 4

METHOD

1. Mix the garlic with the butter or margarine in a small bowl.

2. Spread the bread on one side with the garlic butter. Wrap in foil and bake in a preheated oven at Gas Mark 7, 425°F, 220°C for 15 minutes. Serve hot.

Illustrated opposite

Clockwise from top left: **Crusty bread** (*see above*); **Garlic bread** (*see above*); **Herb dumplings** (*see p. 63*); **Caraway seed toast fingers** (*see p. 66*); **Cheese rusks** (*see p. 66*).

CHEESE RUSKS

INGREDIENTS

4 large thin slices of wholemeal bread
2–4oz (50–125g) Cheddar cheese,
finely grated

•

NUTRITION PROFILE

*These rusks are a good source of Vitamin
B₁₂, calcium and zinc.*

• Per portion •
Carbohydrate: 10.2g
Protein: 8.7g   Fibre: 2.1g
Fat: 9.1g   Calories: 155

*With their crunchy texture and savoury flavour, these rusks make a
good accompaniment to cheesy and vegetable soups and add extra
protein to the first course.*

Preparation time: 10 mins   Cooking time: 20 mins
Serves 4

METHOD

1. Cover the bread slices with the finely grated cheese, pressing
down with a knife.

2. Place on a baking sheet. Bake in a preheated oven at Gas
Mark 6, 400°F, 200°C for 15–20 minutes until crisp and
golden brown.

3. Cut the crusts off the bread, then cut neatly into rectangles
or triangles.

Illustrated on page 65

CARAWAY SEED TOAST FINGERS

INGREDIENTS

4 thin slices of wholemeal bread
1 tbsp (15ml) butter or margarine
2 tsp (10ml) caraway seeds

•

NUTRITION PROFILE

*These toasted fingers contain useful
amounts of iron and zinc.*

• Per portion •
Carbohydrate: 11.4g
Protein: 2.7g   Fibre: 2.2g
Fat: 4.1g   Calories: 90

*These tasty savoury fingers are easy to make and are best served with a
cheesy soup or one containing caraway seeds. Try using fennel or
aniseeds for variation.*

Preparation time: 5 mins   Cooking time: 5 mins
Serves 4

METHOD

1. Remove the crusts from the slices of bread.

2. Butter one side and sprinkle with the caraway seeds.

3. Toast the buttered side under a preheated grill until golden
brown. Cut into fingers and serve immediately.

Illustrated on page 65

GARNISHES

Garnishes add an extra dimension to any dish, providing colour, visual appeal, extra flavour and nutrients. Here are a few ideas for quick and easy last minute additions to soups and starters.

FRESH HERBS

Add a sprig or a sprinkling of finely chopped herbs, parsley or chives to soups or any starter; it boosts the mineral count.

CHEESE

Finely grate some low-fat hard cheese and sprinkle a little on each bowl for added protein.

SAUTÉED VEGETABLES

In hot vegetable soups, sauté a small slice, floret or piece of the main ingredient for the top. This increases the vitamin content.

NUTS

Toast, chop or flake nuts such as almonds, hazelnuts, walnuts or sunflower seeds, for added protein. They are good on soups, pâtés, salads and stuffed vegetables.

YOGURT, SMETANA OR SILKEN TOFU

These are good, low-fat substitutes for cream in soup. Stir the soup and pour a swirl of yogurt or smetana into each bowlful just before serving. Process silken tofu in a blender or food processor before adding.

Illustrated on page 69

SLICED FRUIT

Add a decoratively shaped slice of apple, a twist or some rind of lemon or orange, or a single strawberry to cold or fruity soups, pâtés, fruit starters and dips.

MAKING GARNISHES

Garnishes are an important part of any meal, because they can so dramatically enhance the appearance of a dish. The visual appeal is essential if you are trying to change to healthier eating habits for yourself, family or friends. A sprinkling of herbs, grated cheese or chopped nuts will take no time at all, while more complicated garnishes such as carefully prepared vegetables or fruits, roasted seeds, or wholemeal croûtons take a little longer. But any time spent on a garnish is well-rewarded by the differences to the end result.

1. Use the tip of a sharp knife to split or slice nuts; and a food processor, electric grinder or nut mill to crush them.

2. To make croûtons, dice ½ inch (1cm) thick slices of bread into small squares. Fry, grill or dry-bake until gold.

3. For raw vegetable garnishes, try pepper rings, cauliflower florets or twists of carrot parings.

GOMASHIO

INGREDIENTS

8oz (250g) sesame seeds
³/₄oz (20g) sea salt

•

NUTRITION PROFILE

This garnish is rich in Vitamin B₁ and in niacin, calcium, magnesium, iron, zinc and protein.

• Per portion •
Carbohydrate: 4g
Protein: 16.5g **Fibre:** 2.9g
Fat: 34.3g **Calories:** 370

Gomashio is a sesame seed and sea salt garnish. Sprinkled over soup, grain or vegetable dishes, it adds extra nutrients and lends a nutty flavour to the dish.

Preparation time: 5 mins   Cooking time: 5 mins
Makes approx 9oz (275g)

METHOD

1. Roast the sesame seeds in a dry frying pan over a low heat. Stir continuously so that the seeds roast evenly.

2. When the seeds give off a nutty aroma, have turned a darker shade and start popping, remove from the pan. Grind them in a small electric grinder or food processor together with the salt, until the seeds are half crushed.

3. Cool and store in an airtight container and use within a week.

Illustrated opposite

SEAWEED CONDIMENT

INGREDIENTS

1 strip of wakame or kombu

NUTRITION PROFILE

This condiment is rich in iron, iodine and B Vitamins, but contains no other significant nutrients.

Seaweeds, such as wakame and kombu, are rich in minerals and when ground into a powder make a good garnish for soups.

Preparation time: 5 mins   Cooking time: 5 mins
Serves 4

METHOD

1. Place the seaweed on a baking sheet. Roast in a preheated oven at Gas Mark 5, 375°F, 190°C for 5 minutes or under a preheated grill until crisp. Allow to cool slightly.

2. Break into small pieces and grind to a fine powder in a small electric grinder or food processor. Leave to cool and serve sprinkled on top of soups, particularly miso soup.

Illustrated opposite

From top left to right: **Chopped nuts, hard-boiled egg, raw mushroom, yogurt, raw carrot, chopped parsley, croûtons, grated cheese, sautéed vegetables** (*see p. 67*); **Seaweed condiment** (*see above*); **Gomashio** (*see above*).

STARTERS

Fruits, vegetables and nuts all make nutritious starters. The
following recipes include hot and cold; light and filling; cooked
and chilled starters that can be chosen to combine
nutritionally, visually and in flavour with the rest of the meal.
Many also make good supper dishes, served with a salad.

ASPARAGUS SOUFFLE

INGREDIENTS

1½ lb (750g) fresh asparagus, trimmed
(or 2 × 10oz/300g cans asparagus)
¼ pint (150ml) cooking water (or
liquid from the cans of asparagus)
1½ tsp (7.5ml) agar-agar powder
8 fl oz (250ml) smetana
salt and black pepper
2 egg whites

GARNISH
4 asparagus tips

•

NUTRITION PROFILE

*This starter is low in calories and rich in
Vitamins A, B₁, C, E and folic acid.*

• Per portion •
Carbohydrate: 6.4g
Protein: 12.1g   Fibre: 2.8g
Fat: 5.8g   Calories: 125

*The mild but distinctive flavour of asparagus blends well with a light
soufflé mixture to make a luxurious starter. This recipe uses smetana
instead of cream to keep the fat and calorie content low.*

Preparation time: 25 mins   Cooking time: 30 mins (plus chilling time)
Serves 4

METHOD

1. Tie the fresh asparagus into bundles and stand them upright in
a saucepan of water or steam them in a steamer for about 25
minutes or until tender. Reserve the cooking water.

2. When tender, cut off the tips and mash them thoroughly.
Reserve the stalks to make a stock, or discard. Mix the asparagus
with the cooking water in a saucepan.

3. Sprinkle over the agar-agar powder and bring to the boil,
stirring all the time. Simmer for 1–2 minutes. Cool slightly.

4. Mix the ingredients with the smetana in a blender or food
processor until smooth. Transfer to a bowl and season.

5. Whisk the egg whites until soft peaks form and fold into the
mixture. Dip four individual ramekin dishes in cold water, drain
briefly then pour in the mixture. Chill the soufflés until firm.
Garnish with the asparagus tips before serving.

Illustrated on page 73

SAVOURY CHOUX

INGREDIENTS

CHOUX PASTRY
1oz (25g) soft vegetable margarine
5 tbsp (75ml) cold water
1¼oz (35g) 85% wholemeal flour
1 small egg, beaten
1oz (25g) Cheddar cheese, grated
¼ tsp wholegrain mustard

FILLING
14oz (400g) canned artichoke hearts, drained and finely chopped or mashed
12 capers, finely chopped
4 medium gherkins
1 tsp (5ml) lemon juice

DRESSING
2 fl oz (50ml) smetana
1 tsp (5ml) red wine vinegar

•

NUTRITION PROFILE

This recipe is a good source of Vitamins A, B₁₂ and D.

• Per portion •
Carbohydrate: 8.5g
Protein: 5.4g **Fibre:** 0.7g
Fat: 10g **Calories:** 145

Serve these cheese choux as soon as possible after baking while they are crisp. The piquant filling adds a contrast in texture.

Preparation time: 35 mins   Cooking time: 25 mins
Serves 4

METHOD

1. Make the savoury choux pastry (see below), adding the grated cheese and mustard after the egg.

2. Pipe the mixture on to a greased baking sheet (see below), and bake in a preheated oven at Gas Mark 7, 425°F, 220°C for 15–20 minutes or until the buns are golden and crisp.

3. Cook on the other side (see below) until they are crisp underneath. Cool the buns on a wire rack.

4. For the filling, mix the chopped artichoke hearts with the capers, gherkins and lemon juice. Taste and season if necessary.

5. Make a slit in the buns and fill with some of the mixture. Cool.

6. For the smetana dressing, mix the smetana and vinegar together. Pour the dressing over the buns just before serving.

Illustrated on page 73

MAKING CHOUX

Choux pastry is characterized by its light, airy texture and works well with sweet or savoury fillings. Ideally it should be made, baked and eaten straight away. In its raw state, when it is more like a paste than a pastry, it will keep for 1–2 days in a fridge, but once baked it will lose its crispness fairly quickly.

1. Mix the margarine and water and boil. Remove from the heat and beat in the flour. Gradually add the beaten egg.

2. Pipe dessertspoonfuls of the mixture on to a greased baking sheet. Bake in a preheated oven for 15–20 minutes.

3. Pierce a small hole in the bottom of each choux, turn over and bake for a further 2–3 minutes. Cool on a rack.

SPICED YELLOW PEPPER DIP

INGREDIENTS

1 large yellow pepper, skinned
$^1/_2$ tsp coriander seeds
$^1/_4$–$^1/_2$ tsp mustard seeds
4 sticks white celery, trimmed and
finely chopped
2oz (50g) soft or regular tofu, cubed
2 tsp (10ml) lemon juice
salt and white pepper

GARNISH
ring of yellow pepper or fresh
coriander leaves
•

NUTRITION PROFILE

*This dip is low in fat and calories and a
good source of Vitamin C.*

• Per portion •
Carbohydrate: 1.3g
Protein: 1.2g **Fibre:** 0.7g
Fat: 0.5g **Calories:** 15

*This low-fat dip has an unusual flavour and is good served with crudités
(strips of raw vegetables) before a meal or for a buffet. Pepper skins can
be removed either by baking or grilling. If you prefer to use the grill, be
sure to keep turning the pepper so that only the outer skin blisters.*

Preparation time: 20 mins   Cooking time: 20 mins
Serves 4

METHOD

1. Put the yellow pepper in a preheated oven at Gas Mark 5,
375°F, 190°C for 20 minutes or until the skin comes off easily.

2. Fry the coriander and mustard seeds gently in an ungreased
frying pan until they turn a shade darker.

3. Halve and deseed the pepper, then chop it into small pieces
and mix with the celery, tofu, coriander seeds, mustard seeds and
lemon juice in a blender or food processor until smooth.

4. Taste and adjust the seasoning. Pour the mixture into a small
bowl and leave to cool thoroughly. Garnish and serve with a
variety of crudités (see p.67).

Illustrated opposite

CHILLED GRAPEFRUIT WITH MINT

INGREDIENTS

2 grapefruits
2 pink grapefruits
2 oranges

GLAZE
2 tsp (10ml) arrowroot
2 tsp (10ml) clear honey
2 tsp (10ml) sesame or poppy seeds

GARNISH
sprigs of fresh mint or sweet cicely
•

NUTRITION PROFILE

*This low-calorie, low-fat starter is rich in
Vitamin C.*

• Per portion •
Carbohydrate: 18.5g
Protein: 2.3g **Fibre:** 3.5g
Fat: 1.4g **Calories:** 90

*A honey and sesame seed glaze brings sweetness to the acid fruit. If you
like your grapefruit even sweeter, try adding some chopped cicely leaves.*

Preparation time: 25 mins   Cooking time: 5 mins
Serves 4

METHOD

1. Cut the grapefruits and oranges in half. Cut into segments,
between the membranes. Reserve the juice and spoon the
segments into 4 grapefruit shells.

2. For the glaze, mix the arrowroot with the reserved fruit juice.
Add the honey. Bring the mixture to the boil and simmer for 1–2
minutes. Cool slightly. Pour over the fruit and leave to cool.

3. Meanwhile, toast the seeds under a grill until they start to
jump. Sprinkle over the fruit. Garnish and serve chilled.

Illustrated on page 74

Clockwise from top left: **Savoury choux** (*see p.71*); **Asparagus soufflé** (*see p.70*); **Spiced yellow pepper dip** (*see above*).

NUT PATE

INGREDIENTS

¹/₂oz (15g) butter or margarine
1 small onion, peeled and chopped
2 large mushrooms, wiped and chopped
1 large tomato, skinned and chopped
¹/₂ tbsp (7.5ml) wholemeal flour
3 fl oz (75ml) stock or water
1 tsp (5ml) yeast extract
1 tsp (5ml) chopped fresh mixed herbs
2oz (50g) hazelnuts
1oz (25g) unsalted cashew nuts
1oz (25g) almonds
2oz (50g) wholemeal breadcrumbs
1 egg, beaten

GLAZE
¹/₂ tsp agar-agar powder
¹/₂ tsp yeast extract

GARNISH
slices of tomato

•

NUTRITION PROFILE

*This pâté is rich in iron and magnesium
and Vitamins B₁, C and E and niacin.*

• Per portion •
Carbohydrate: 15.4g
Protein: 7.8g **Fibre:** 4g
Fat: 15.4g **Calories:** 230

*This mixed nut pâté makes a nutritious and filling starter. It is equally
good for picnics and packed lunches as it has a firm texture and
transports well.*

Preparation time: 30 mins   Cooking time: 45–50 mins
Serves 4

METHOD

1. Melt the butter in a saucepan and gently fry the onion
until soft.

2. Add the mushrooms and cook for a further 2–3 minutes. Stir in
the tomato, cover and simmer for 5 minutes.

3. Sprinkle the flour over the mixture and cook for 2–3 minutes,
stirring. Add the stock, yeast extract and mixed herbs and cook
for another 5 minutes.

4. Meanwhile, grind the nuts in a food processor or electric
grinder. Add to the vegetable mixture, together with the
breadcrumbs. Mix in the egg and season to taste. Leave to stand
for 10 minutes.

5. Pack the mixture in a terrine and cook (see below).

6. Make the agar-agar glaze (see below), glaze the pâté and leave
to cool thoroughly. Serve garnished with slices of tomato.

Illustrated opposite

MAKING PATE

*Pâté is the French word for a meat or fish pie, although it has come to mean a spread rather than a pie. It can
be served hot or cold. A vegetarian pâté makes a good replacement for the meat portion in a conventional
meal and will provide plenty of protein and fibre because of the bean, nut, vegetable or cheese base.*

1. Mix up the ingredients as directed in
the recipe you are using. Leave to stand
for 10 minutes.

2. Pack into a terrine, cover with
greased paper and foil. Steam for 45–50
minutes. When cool, turn out.

3. Dissolve agar-agar powder in water,
simmer for 1–2 minutes then add yeast
extract. Pour over the pâté.

Top: **Chilled grapefruit with mint** (*see p.72*); Bottom: **Nut pâté** (*see above*).

FROSTED TOMATO COCKTAIL

INGREDIENTS

¾ pint (450ml) tomato juice
1 tbsp (15ml) chopped fresh mint
1 tsp (5ml) lemon juice
1 tsp (5ml) tamari or shoyu

GARNISH
few sprigs of mint

•

NUTRITION PROFILE

This fat-free, low-calorie starter is a good source of Vitamins A and C.

• Per portion •
Carbohydrate: 3.8g
Protein: 0.8g **Fibre:** --
Fat: -- **Calories:** 20

This tomato water ice, flavoured with lemon and mint, makes a refreshing, low-calorie start to a summer meal. It is also quick, easy and cheap to prepare.

Preparation time: 5 mins (plus 4½ hours' freezing and softening time)
Serves 4

METHOD

1. Mix together the tomato juice, chopped mint, lemon juice and tamari in a bowl or jug. Transfer into a freezerproof container. Cover and freeze for about 4 hours until solid.

2. Remove the water ice from the freezer and leave at room temperature for 20–30 minutes to soften slightly. Then crush the ice finely.

3. Pile the crushed tomato ice into individual dishes or glasses. Garnish with sprigs of mint and serve at once.

Illustrated opposite

MELON ᴬᴺᴰ GINGER SORBET

INGREDIENTS

½ honeydew melon
½ cantaloupe melon
½ tsp ground ginger
⅛ tsp ground cinnamon
juice of 1 lime
2 egg whites

GARNISH
lime rind

•

NUTRITION PROFILE

This low-calorie, fat-free starter is rich in Vitamins A and C.

• Per portion •
Carbohydrate: 6.5g
Protein: 0.6g **Fibre:** 1.2g
Fat: -- **Calories:** 30

This sweet yet sharp sorbet, with its light, soft texture helps to stimulate the appetite. Extremely low in calories, it makes a light starter.

Preparation time: 30 mins (plus about 4 hours' freezing time)
Cooking time: 15 mins
Serves 6–8

METHOD

1. Remove the seeds from the melons and scoop out the flesh. Coarsely chop the flesh and place in a saucepan with the ginger, cinnamon and lime juice. Cover and cook over a low heat for 10–15 minutes or until the melon is soft. Cool slightly.

2. Purée the cooked melon in a blender or food processor until smooth and pour into a freezerproof bowl. Freeze for about 2 hours.

3. Whisk the egg whites until stiff, whisk the melon purée, then fold the whites into the purée. Transfer to a shallow, freezerproof container. Return the purée to the freezer for at least 2 hours.

4. Serve in individual dishes and garnish with curls of lime rind.

Illustrated opposite

Clockwise from top: **Individual vegetable terrines en gêlée** (*see p. 78*); **Frosted tomato cocktail** (*see above*); **Melon and ginger sorbet** (*see above*).

INDIVIDUAL VEGETABLE TERRINES EN GELEE

INGREDIENTS

FIRST LAYER
2 large red peppers
salt and black pepper

SECOND LAYER
¼ cucumber, finely diced
½ avocado, peeled and creamed
1 tsp (5ml) lemon juice
1 tbsp (15ml) toasted pine kernels,
chopped
½ tsp chopped fresh lovage
1 tsp (5ml) chopped fresh parsley
or chervil

THIRD LAYER
8oz (250g) carrots, diced
1 tbsp (15ml) fresh orange juice

JELLY
1 tsp (5ml) agar-agar powder
½ pint (300ml) cold water

GARNISH
4 sprigs of lovage, parsley or chervil
•

NUTRITION PROFILE

*This low-calorie starter is a good source of
Vitamins A, C and E.*

• Per portion •
Carbohydrate: 7.3g
Protein: 2.5g   **Fibre:** 2.9g
Fat: 7g   **Calories:** 100

*The setting agent agar-agar is very easy to use as it can be remelted any
number of times. These terrines are light and have an agreeable
combination of different textures and colours. To vary the recipe,
substitute mashed cauliflower for the carrots. If you prefer, you can
make one large, loaf-shaped terrine instead of four individual ones.*

Preparation time: 50 mins (plus setting time)   Cooking time: 40 mins
Serves 4

METHOD

1. For the first layer, put the red peppers in an ovenproof dish.
Bake in a preheated oven at Gas Mark 6–7, 400–425°F,
200–220°C, for 30 minutes or until the peppers are tender
and the skins peel off easily.

2. Cut the peppers in half and remove the white pith and the seeds.
Dry well with absorbent kitchen paper. Dice the pepper flesh.
Purée in a blender or food processor. Season and leave to cool.

3. For the second layer, mix the diced cucumber with the
creamed avocado. Add the lemon juice, chopped pine kernels
and herbs. Season to taste.

4. For the third layer, cook the carrots in a saucepan of boiling
water until tender. Drain and either chop very finely or mix in a
blender or food processor until roughly mashed. Add the orange
juice, season to taste, and leave to cool.

5. Place a sprig of lovage, chervil or parsley at the bottom of four
individual ramekin dishes.

6. Dissolve the agar-agar in the cold water. Bring to the boil and
simmer for 1–2 minutes. Pour a thin layer on top of each sprig of
herbs and leave to set. Then pour in a little more of the liquid,
tilting each dish from side to side so that its sides are coated with a
layer of jelly. Leave to set in a cool place.

7. When cold and set, spoon a layer of red pepper purée on top of it.
Cover with a thin layer of reheated agar-agar jelly and leave to set.

8. When completely cold, add the cucumber layer. As before,
seal with a thin layer of reheated agar-agar jelly, and leave to set.

9. Add the carrot layer. Seal with a final layer of agar-agar jelly,
and leave to set in the fridge until completely cold.

10. Push a knife down both sides of the terrines and turn out
carefully. Serve with any leftover red pepper purée.

Illustrated on page 77

MUSHROOM AND WATERCRESS PATE
WITH JUNIPER BERRIES

INGREDIENTS

¼oz (7g) butter or margarine
½ onion, peeled and finely chopped
8oz (250g) dark mushrooms, wiped
10 juniper berries, crushed
pinch salt
4oz (125g) watercress, chopped
2 tbsp (30ml) water
2oz (50g) shelled pecan nuts, ground
(or 1½oz/40g ground walnuts)
salt and black pepper

•

NUTRITION PROFILE

This low-calorie pâté is rich in copper, folic acid, Vitamins A and C and niacin.

• Per portion •
Carbohydrate: 1.2g
Protein: 3.2g **Fibre:** 3.3g
Fat: 7.6g **Calories:** 85

This smooth, light pâté makes a good low-calorie starter on toast. The slightly resinous-tasting juniper berries complement the pervading flavours of mushroom and watercress.

Preparation time: 15 mins   Cooking time: 25 mins
Serves 4

METHOD

1. Melt the butter in a covered saucepan and gently fry the onion until soft. Add the mushrooms, juniper berries and salt and cook for a further 5 minutes.

2. Stir in the watercress and cook for a further 2–3 minutes. Then add the water and cook for 10 minutes. Cool, then chop the mixture very finely. Add the pecan nuts and seasoning. Mix well and put in a serving dish. Allow to cool completely.

3. Serve on individual plates on a bed of lettuce or watercress with wholemeal or melba toast.

Illustrated on page 80

CHICK PEA AND TAHINI DIP

INGREDIENTS

2oz (50g) chick peas, soaked
2 tbsp (30ml) tahini
4 fl oz (125ml) stock
2 tbsp (30ml) lemon juice
1 tsp (5ml) olive oil
1 tsp (5ml) shoyu
1–2 cloves garlic, crushed
salt and black pepper

•

NUTRITION PROFILE

This appetizer is a good source of magnesium.

• Per portion •
Carbohydrate: 6.8g
Protein: 4.8g **Fibre:** 2.1g
Fat: 6.8g **Calories:** 105

Often known as hummus, this dip has a strong Middle Eastern flavour of chick peas, lemon juice and tahini. The consistency should be thick enough to coat the accompanying crudités (strips of raw vegetables).

Preparation time: 25 mins (plus 12 hours' minimum soaking)
Cooking time: 1 hour
Serves 4

METHOD

1. Drain the chick peas and place in a saucepan of fresh water. Bring to the boil and boil fast for 10 minutes, then simmer for another 50 minutes until soft and easy to mash.

2. Drain and then mash the chick peas with either a potato masher or in a blender or food processor while still warm. Add the tahini, stock, lemon juice, olive oil, shoyu, garlic and seasoning and mix well. Transfer to a serving dish and cool.

3. Meanwhile, cut the chosen vegetables into julienne strips, slices or florets. Arrange them around the dip and serve.

Illustrated on page 80

MARINATED AUBERGINE

INGREDIENTS

1 lb (500g) aubergine
¼ pint (150ml) water
½ pint (300ml) white wine vinegar

MARINADE

1 tbsp (15ml) lemon juice
2 tbsp (30ml) olive oil
2 cloves garlic, crushed
2 tsp (10ml) chopped fresh oregano
1 tsp (5ml) chopped green chilli
1 tbsp (15ml) capers
salt and black pepper

•

NUTRITION PROFILE

*This low-calorie starter is a good
source of Vitamin C.*

• Per portion •
Carbohydrate: 4.6g
Protein: 1g **Fibre:** 3.1g
Fat: 3.8g **Calories:** 55

*This is a healthy adaptation of a rich traditional Italian recipe. It makes
a strongly flavoured starter with a surprisingly smooth texture.*

Preparation time: 20 mins (plus 24 hours' marinating)
Cooking time: about 10 mins
Serves 4

METHOD

1. Peel and thinly slice the aubergine lengthways.

2. Mix the water and vinegar together in a covered saucepan, and
bring to the boil. Add a few slices of aubergine at a time to the
pan and simmer until the colour and texture begin to change.
Drain and repeat the process until all the slices are cooked.

3. For the marinade, mix all the ingredients together in a jar. Add
the warm aubergine and leave to marinate for 24 hours.

4. Drain and serve cool with warm, wholemeal toast.

Illustrated opposite

HERB GNOCCHI

INGREDIENTS

2oz (50g) fresh watercress or
dandelion leaves
2oz (50g) sorrel
4oz (125g) spinach leaves
½oz (15g) fresh parsley
2 tsp (10ml) fresh tarragon,
finely chopped
2 tsp (10ml) fresh marjoram,
finely chopped
2oz (50g) ricotta cheese
2oz (50g) curd cheese
1 small egg, beaten
1½oz (40g) semolina

•

NUTRITION PROFILE

*This recipe is a good source of Vitamins A,
B₁, B₁₂, C, folic acid, iron and calcium.*

• Per portion •
Carbohydrate: 7.7g
Protein: 8.6g **Fibre:** 4g
Fat: 6.8g **Calories:** 125

*This is a low-fat version of Italian gnocchi. Here the semolina
dumplings are flavoured with spinach, watercress and fresh herbs.*

Preparation time: 25 mins   Cooking time: 25 mins
Serves 4–5

METHOD

1. Wash and steam the watercress or dandelion leaves, sorrel,
spinach and parsley together for 6–10 minutes. Drain and dry
well, chop finely, then place in a bowl and stir in the herbs.

2. Mix together the ricotta cheese, curd cheese and egg in a
separate bowl. Mix well and add to the chopped herbs and
vegetables. Stir in the semolina and leave to cool thoroughly.

3. Bring a saucepan of water to the boil. Gently drop 4–6
dessertspoonfuls of the mixture at a time into the simmering water
and cook until the gnocchi rise to the surface.

4. Remove from the pan using a slotted spoon and place on a
serving dish. Sprinkle on some Parmesan cheese and serve hot.

Illustrated on page 83

Clockwise from top: **Chick pea and tahini dip** (*see p.79*); **Marinated aubergine** (*see above*);
Mushroom and watercress pâté with juniper berries (*see p.79*).

CHICORY WITH YOGURT HOLLANDAISE SAUCE

INGREDIENTS

4 heads of chicory (about 1 lb/500g
in weight)
1 tsp (5ml) butter or margarine
salt and black pepper
4 spinach or 4 large sorrel leaves

SAUCE
2 tbsp (30ml) wine vinegar
4 black peppercorns
1 bay leaf
1 blade mace
2 egg yolks
4 fl oz (125ml) natural yogurt

•

NUTRITION PROFILE

*This recipe is low-calorie and a good source
of Vitamins B_{12}, C and D and of iron and
folic acid.*

• Per portion •
Carbohydrate: 3.8g
Protein: 6g   **Fibre:** 2.9g
Fat: 7.4g   **Calories:** 105

This hollandaise sauce, which uses yogurt instead of butter, is a low-calorie version of the traditional recipe. Take care not to overheat the sauce or it will curdle. Serve warm.

Preparation time: 25 mins   Cooking time: 1 hour
Serves 4

METHOD

1. Trim the stems of the chicory and discard any wilted outside leaves. Arrange in a lightly buttered ovenproof dish. Season.

2. Cover and bake in a preheated oven at Gas Mark 4, 350°F, 180°C for 50 minutes. Roll each chicory head in a spinach or sorrel leaf, cover with foil and cook for a further 10 minutes.

3. For the hollandaise sauce, mix the wine vinegar, peppercorns, bay leaf and mace in a saucepan and bring to the boil. Continue boiling until the liquid has reduced to 2 tsp (10ml).

4. Beat the egg yolks in a small bowl. Strain the reduced vinegar into them. Put the bowl over a pan of hot water and heat gently, stirring constantly, until thickened. Add the yogurt, season and continue stirring until the sauce coats the back of the spoon.

5. Drain the chicory and serve with the sauce poured over.

Illustrated opposite

EGGS FLORENTINE

INGREDIENTS

1 tsp (5ml) butter or margarine
8 spinach leaves, chopped in strips
4 fl oz (125ml) smetana
4 eggs
salt and black pepper

GARNISH
chopped fresh parsley

•

NUTRITION PROFILE

*This starter is rich in calcium and Vitamins
A, B_{12} and D.*

• Per portion •
Carbohydrate: 1.7g
Protein: 8.1g   **Fibre:** 0.6g
Fat: 9.4g   **Calories:** 125

Served in ramekin dishes surrounded by small wholemeal toasts, this simple recipe makes an attractive and nutritious dinner party starter.

Preparation time: 10 mins   Cooking time: 25 mins
Serves 4

METHOD

1. Grease 4 ramekin dishes with the butter. Divide half the spinach and put into the base of each ramekin dish. Add 1 tsp (5ml) smetana and break an egg into each.

2. Arrange the rest of the spinach over the egg whites and cover with the rest of the smetana, leaving the yolks bare. Season.

3. Bake in a preheated oven at Gas Mark 4, 350°F, 180°C for 25 minutes or until the egg is just about to set. Serve immediately.

Illustrated opposite

Clockwise from top left: **Eggs florentine** (*see above*); **Chicory with yogurt hollandaise sauce** (*see above*); **Herb gnocchi** (*see p. 81*).

ONION PIZZA TART

INGREDIENTS

DOUGH
1 tsp (5ml) fresh yeast
3 tbsp (45ml) warm water
1 small egg, beaten
4oz (125g) wholemeal flour
½ tsp salt

TOPPING
1 tbsp (15ml) olive oil
2 large onions, peeled and
finely chopped
2 tsp (10ml) chopped fresh basil
salt and black pepper
4 tomatoes, sliced
16 black olives, stoned
black pepper
12 fresh basil leaves

•

NUTRITION PROFILE

*This starter is a good source of magnesium,
iron, folic acid and Vitamins B and C.*

• Per portion •
Carbohydrate: 28.5g
Protein: 7.5g **Fibre:** 6g
Fat: 7.1g **Calories:** 200

*Sometimes known as pissaladière, this French dish is a cross between
onion tart and pizza. This low-fat version is light enough to be served as
a starter before a salad or vegetable main course. If you do not have
basil, try using oregano or marjoram instead.*

Preparation time: 30 mins (plus 35 mins rising time for the dough)
Cooking time: 40–55 mins
Serves 4

METHOD

1. Mix the yeast with the warm water. Leave to stand for 5
minutes in a warm place.

2. Add the beaten egg to the yeast mixture. Put the flour and salt
in a bowl and make a well in the centre. Add the yeast mixture
and mix together to a soft dough (add extra water if necessary.)

3. Turn the dough on to a floured board and knead for 5 minutes
until smooth and elastic.

4. Transfer the dough to a clean bowl. Cover with clingfilm and
leave to rise for 35 minutes in a warm place.

5. For the topping, heat the oil in a saucepan and fry the onions
on a low heat for 20–25 minutes until soft and almost puréed.
Add the chopped basil and seasoning.

6. When the dough has risen, knock it back and knead lightly.
Roll out the dough to fit a greased 8 inch (20cm) flan ring. Push
the dough well into the sides.

7. Spread over the onion mixture. Arrange the tomatoes on top
and add the olives in a decorative pattern. Season with pepper.

8. Leave to prove for a further 10–15 minutes. Bake in a
preheated oven at Gas Mark 5, 375°F, 190°C for 20–30 minutes.

9. When cooked, cool slightly and arrange the fresh basil leaves
on top. Serve hot or warm.

Illustrated on page 86

RICOTTA ROULADE

INGREDIENTS

6oz (175g) Swiss chard leaves (or spinach)
1 tsp (5ml) made mustard
3 eggs, separated
salt and black pepper

FILLING
6oz (175g) fresh ricotta cheese, mashed

GARNISH
sprig of coriander

•

NUTRITION PROFILE

This starter is a good source of Vitamins A, B₁₂, C and D, folic acid, calcium and iron.

• Per portion •
Carbohydrate: 1.1g
Protein: 11.5g   **Fibre:** 2.8g
Fat: 11.9g   **Calories:** 155

Swiss chard leaves, otherwise known as sea kale, are rich in iron and have a strong flavour that balances well with ricotta cheese.

Preparation time: 35 mins   Cooking time: 15–20 mins
Serves 4

METHOD

1. Wash the Swiss chard thoroughly. Put it in a saucepan with only the water on its leaves and cook for about 10 minutes.

2. When cooked, cool slightly and drain thoroughly. Chop the leaves as finely as possible. Transfer the chopped leaves to a mixing bowl and add the mustard and egg yolks. Carefully fold the stiffly whisked egg whites into the mixture.

3. Prepare the roulade (see below), and bake in a preheated oven at Gas Mark 6, 400°F, 200°C for 15–20 minutes or until golden brown and starts shrinking from the sides of the tin.

4. Leave to cool for 2–3 minutes, then turn it out, cover with the mashed ricotta and roll up (see below).

5. Reduce the oven to Gas Mark 5, 375°F, 190°C and reheat the roulade quickly for 5 minutes.

6. Trim off the ends and serve in slices.
Illustrated on page 86

MAKING A ROULADE

The word 'roulade' literally means a roll, and this dish can be sweet or savoury, served hot or cold. Savoury roulades are traditionally stuffed rolls of meat or fish, but vegetables or cheese work just as well. A roulade is usually bound together by eggs, then baked and rolled in the same way as a Swiss roll.

1. Fold the egg whites into the leaf, mustard and yolk mixture. Pour into a Swiss roll tin, bake for 15–20 minutes.

2. Leave to cool for 2–3 minutes. Turn out on to a sheet of greaseproof paper and carefully peel off the lining paper.

3. Coat the top of the roulade with the filling and roll up. Transfer to an ovenproof dish and bake for 5 minutes.

STUFFED MUSHROOMS

INGREDIENTS

4 large flat mushrooms, wiped
1 tbsp (15ml) olive oil
3–4 shallots or 1 small onion, peeled and finely chopped
1 clove garlic, crushed
8oz (250g) large flat mushrooms, chopped
5 tbsp (75ml) red wine
½ tsp dried thyme
1 tbsp (15ml) tomato purée

GARNISH
sprig of parsley
•

NUTRITION PROFILE

This low-calorie starter is rich in copper, niacin and Vitamin B₂.

• Per portion •
Carbohydrate: 3.9g
Protein: 2.3g **Fibre:** 2.4g
Fat: 5g **Calories:** 80

These stuffed mushrooms, filled with a classic 'Duxelles' sauce of mushrooms, wine, shallots or onions, make a light starter.

Preparation time: 25 mins   Cooking time: 20–25 mins
Serves 4

METHOD

1. Remove the stalks from the 4 large mushrooms and chop the stalks finely. Put the caps on one side. Heat 2 tsp (10ml) of the oil in a medium-sized frying pan and fry the stalks, onion, garlic and chopped mushrooms for 5–10 minutes or until very soft.

2. Mix in the red wine and thyme and continue cooking until the wine has almost evaporated. Stir in the tomato purée and seasoning and cook for a further 2–3 minutes.

3. Place the flat mushroom caps in a greased dish. Brush the rest of the oil on to the caps, and pile on the filling. Bake in a preheated oven at Gas Mark 5, 375°F, 190°C for 20–25 minutes.

Illustrated opposite

SPICED PANCAKES

INGREDIENTS

BATTER
1½oz (40g) wholemeal flour
¼ pint (150ml) semi-skimmed milk
1 small egg, size 6, beaten
1 tsp (5ml) oil

FILLING
6oz (175g) fennel or celery, chopped
6oz (175g) leeks, chopped
2oz (50g) curd cheese
4 fl oz (125ml) smetana
6 cardamom seeds
½ tsp fenugreek seeds
•

NUTRITION PROFILE

This recipe is a good source of calcium, Vitamins B₁₂, C and E.

• Per portion •
Carbohydrate: 14.5g
Protein: 9.5g **Fibre:** 5g
Fat: 10.4g **Calories:** 185

These thin, light pancakes have a low-fat, creamy filling flavoured with unusual curry spices.

Preparation time: 30 mins (plus 2 hours' standing time for the batter)
Cooking time: 8 mins
Serves 4

METHOD

1. For the batter, mix all the ingredients together in a blender or food processor to form a thick, smooth mixture. Leave to stand for 1–2 hours.

2. For the filling, steam the fennel and leeks for 6–10 minutes until tender. Whisk the curd cheese and smetana until airy. Toast the seeds in a dry frying pan, crush them and fold into the smetana mixture, then add the steamed vegetables.

3. Make 4 thin pancakes and set them aside. When cooked, fold them in half and then fold over so that they form a cornet. Fill and garnish with flaked almonds.

Illustrated on page 89

Clockwise from top left: **Ricotta roulade** (*see p. 85*); **Stuffed mushrooms** (*see above*); **Onion pizza tart** (*see p. 84*).

AUBERGINE CHARLOTTE

INGREDIENTS

3 small aubergines (about
1–1¼ lb/500–625g in weight)
1 tsp (5ml) salt
2 tbsp (30ml) olive oil
1 medium onion, peeled and finely
chopped
1 clove garlic, crushed
2 tsp (10ml) fresh basil
8 tomatoes, skinned and chopped
salt and black pepper
1 × 10oz (300g) packet silken tofu (or
½ pint/300ml natural set yogurt)
1 tsp (5ml) ground cumin

GARNISH

1oz (25g) shelled walnuts or pecans,
finely chopped

•

NUTRITION PROFILE

*This high-fibre starter is rich in iron,
copper, calcium and folic acid and in
Vitamins C and E.*

• Per portion •
Carbohydrate: 10.6g
Protein: 6.7g **Fibre:** 5.9g
Fat: 13g **Calories:** 190

*This recipe makes an impressive layered galette, which can taste even
better cold than hot. Silken tofu makes a delicious smooth filling, but if
unobtainable, use ½ pint (300ml) natural set yogurt.*

Preparation time: 50 mins   Cooking time: 50 mins
Serves 4

METHOD

1. Trim the aubergines and cut the flesh into ½ inch (1cm) slices.
Sprinkle them with salt and leave for 30 minutes to get rid of the
excess bitter juices. Rinse with cold water and dry thoroughly.

2. Heat 2 tsp (10ml) olive oil in a saucepan and fry the onion
until soft. Add the garlic and basil and cook for a further
2–3 minutes.

3. Stir in the tomatoes. Cook for 20–25 minutes until the
mixture resembles a thick pulp. Season to taste.

4. Brush one side of the aubergine slices with oil and cook under a
preheated grill until golden brown. Turn them over and cook on
the other side. Leave to cool.

5. Mix the tofu and cumin together in a blender until smooth.

6. Grease a 2 pint (1.2 litre) capacity charlotte mould or a 7 inch
(18cm) round cake tin, and arrange a layer of overlapping
aubergine slices at the bottom of the dish.

7. Reserve a third of the tomato mixture. Spread some of the
remaining tomato mixture over the aubergines, sprinkle with
some walnuts, then add some of the tofu mixture. Repeat the
layers finishing with a layer of aubergine slices.

8. Cover the mould with foil and bake in a preheated oven at Gas
Mark 4, 350°F, 180°C for 40–50 minutes or until the tofu is set
and the aubergines are tender.

9. Cool in the dish and turn out when required. Serve with the
remaining tomato sauce spooned over and garnished with
chopped nuts.

Illustrated opposite

Top: **Aubergine Charlotte** (*see above*); Bottom: **Spiced pancakes** (*see p. 87*).